EMBRACING CONTENTMENT IN THE MIDST OF
CAREGIVING, GRIEF, HEARTACHE, AND LOSS

God's Grace Keeps Pace

Pam Whitley Taylor

God's Grace Keeps Pace
Trilogy Christian Publishers A Wholly Owned Subsidiary of Trinity Broadcasting Network
2442 Michelle Drive Tustin, CA 92780
Copyright © 2022 by Pam Whitley Taylor
Scripture quotations marked AMP are taken from the Amplified® Bible (AMP), Copyright © 2015 by The Lockman Foundation. Used by permission. www.Lockman.org. Scripture quotations marked ESV are taken from the ESV® Bible (The Holy Bible, English Standard Version®), copyright © 2001 by Crossway Bibles, a publishing ministry of Good News Publishers. Used by permission. All rights reserved. Scripture quotations marked MSG are taken from THE MESSAGE, copyright © 1993, 2002, 2018 by Eugene H. Peterson. Used by permission of NavPress. All rights reserved. Represented by Tyndale House Publishers, Inc. Scripture quotations marked NASB are taken from the New American Standard Bible® (NASB), Copyright © 1960, 1962, 1963, 1968, 1971, 1972, 1973, 1975, 1977, 1995 by The Lockman Foundation. Used by permission. www.Lockman.org. Scripture quotations marked NIV are taken from the Holy Bible, New International Version®, NIV®. Copyright © 1973, 1978, 1984, 2011 by Biblica, Inc.TM Used by permission of Zondervan. All rights reserved worldwide. www.zondervan.com. The "NIV" and "New International Version" are trademarks registered in the United States Patent and Trademark Office by Biblica, Inc. TM Scripture quotations marked NKJV are taken from the New King James Version®. Copyright © 1982 by Thomas Nelson. Used by permission. All rights reserved. Scripture quotations marked NLT are taken from the Holy Bible, New Living Translation, copyright © 1996, 2004, 2015 by Tyndale House Foundation. Used by permission of Tyndale House Publishers, Inc., Carol Stream, Illinois 60188. All rights reserved. Scripture quotations marked TLB are taken from The Living Bible copyright © 1971. Used by permission of Tyndale House Publishers, a Division of Tyndale House Ministries, Carol Stream, Illinois 60188. All rights reserved. Scripture quotations marked KJV are taken from the King James Version of the Bible. Public domain.
No part of this book may be reproduced, stored in a retrieval system, or transmitted by any means without written permission from the author. All rights reserved. Printed in the USA.
Rights Department, 2442 Michelle Drive, Tustin, CA 92780.
Trilogy Christian Publishing/TBN and colophon are trademarks of Trinity Broadcasting Network.
For information about special discounts for bulk purchases, please contact Trilogy Christian Publishing.
Trilogy Disclaimer: The views and content expressed in this book are those of the author and may not necessarily reflect the views and doctrine of Trilogy Christian Publishing or the Trinity Broadcasting Network.
Manufactured in the United States of America
10 9 8 7 6 5 4 3 2 1
Library of Congress Cataloging-in-Publication Data is available.
ISBN: 978-1-68556-849-8
E-ISBN: 978-1-68556-850-4

Know therefore that the Lord your God is God; he is the faithful God, keeping his covenant of love to a thousand generations of those who love him and keep his commandments.

Deuteronomy 7:9 (NIV)

ACKNOWLEDGMENTS

I want to thank each person that helped me complete this book. Thank you, John, for listening to me read various chapters and giving me extra insight on wording! Thank you, Stephanie, for faithfully pouring over the entire book and giving suggestions, edits, and insights. They were invaluable. Thank you, Angie, Gay, and Pat, for reading and encouraging me all along this path. Thank you, Nika Maples, for your wonderful, encouraging course that inspired me to write. A special thank you also goes to Sue Ferguson and Paula Hemingway, who have been my writing buddies since 2004. You've been such a blessing.

And from the beginning of this hard journey, many precious people have helped and, at times, have held up my arms. I want to say a huge thank you to each of you—you loved us and cheered us on. I call you my angels by my side (listed at the end of the book, on page 248). Thank you!

My 70 birthday party

ENDORSEMENTS

It's a rare treasure to be able to soak up the life stories of the people of God who have trusted and walked with Him through unbearable sorrow to find lasting joy. Pam invited me into her life and story and taught me generosity, curiosity, and gentle trust. Through this book, she will do the same for you, so soak it up. These lessons truly are treasures.

—Jamy Fisher
Pastor's Wife and Bible Teacher

Heartbreak, grief, and sorrow come in many shapes and sizes, and they affect our emotions in various ways. Some last a few hours, some a few days, and some, at least for me, have lasted forty-three years. I'm excited to share with you "God's Grace Keeps Pace" is not only 1000 percent true, but the personal trials of the author, Pam Whitley Taylor, prove that by God's grace, "I can remain confident that I shall look upon the goodness of the Lord in the land of the living."

—Darlene McDaniel
Event Coordinator NAMB—Retired
Mom and Caregiver to Kelly

Pam Whitley Taylor is a prolific author and blogger. Her book, "God's Grace Keeps Pace," shares not only the tragedies and triumphs of her life but reveals the heart of a true God seeker and God follower.

—Louise Tucker Jones
Gold Medallion Award-Winning Author, Speaker

If you have ever felt overwhelmed, alone, or abandoned, I believe Pam's story of God's unfailing love will help you to lean in so close to the Lord that you will truly feel His loving arms lifting you back up!

—Margolyn Woods Andrews
Former Rose Bowl Queen, Speaker, and Author

Table of Contents

Chapter 1: Amazing Grace...11

Chapter 2: There's a Sweet, Sweet Spirit.....................23

Chapter 3: Great Is Thy Faithfulness.........................35

Chapter 4: Sweetly Broken..45

Chapter 5: Masterpiece..51

Chapter 6: Jesus, Take the Wheel...............................63

Chapter 7: My Weapon..75

Chapter 8: Praise You in the Storm..........................85

Chapter 9: Keep Walkin'..93

Chapter 10: I Am a Promise...107

Chapter 11: There Was Jesus......................................119

Chapter 12: Rescue...133

Chapter 13: Cry Out to Jesus......................................139

Chapter 14: How Great Is Our God............................151

Chapter 15: Send the Light..163

Chapter 16: God Will Make a Way..............................181

Chapter 17: In the Eye of the Storm.........................191

Chapter 18: Count Your Blessings............................201

Chapter 19: Jesus Loves Me......................................215

Chapter 20: The Anchor Holds.................................231

Chapter 21: It Is Well with My Soul........................237

Chapter 22: When I'm Gone....................................257

Chapter 23: The Mercy Tree....................................277

Angels by My Side 285

Chapter 1
AMAZING GRACE

"Our days may come to seventy years, or eighty, if our strength endures; yet the best of them are but trouble and sorrow, for they quickly pass, and we fly away" (Psalm 90:10, NIV).

As I look back over my seventy years of living, I have a treasure trove of wonderful memories, but intertwined in their midst, are many hard and painful ones as well. It amazes me that together they form a beautiful tapestry of my life. The dark tear-stained strands of pain are skillfully woven with vibrantly colored ones of His joy and His teaching—His wonderful provision and grace shine from every tender and throbbing place I walk, and I see His presence in the midst of it all. Like Job 42:5 (NLT), "[I can say,] I had only heard about you before, but now I have seen you with my own eyes" (hereinafter, brackets added for clarity).

I grew up in the nineteen fifties gazing at beautiful Mississippi skies, fascinated by the big and little dipper that shimmered above me at night. By day, I was captivated by the clouds, studying them carefully as I searched for special shapes all the while pondering about God and His heavens.

Our front porch swing was my favorite perch to watch the sun as its royal beauty disappeared below the horizon. I was never tired of God's masterpiece repainted each evening.

And as darkness overtook our hilltop home, I listened with delight as the crickets and katydids began their evening songs. Their chirps seemed to crescendo across the hollow as the night grew darker and their lively melodies blended with the sounds of bobwhites and whippoor-will—their lonesome-sounding songs calling across the woods to one another. The countryside further came alive as hundreds of fireflies (or lightning bugs, as I called them) transformed our woods and yard into a magical oasis of twinkling beauty.

In my childhood years, I loved to explore our small farm accompanied by my dogs Fido and King, skipping through the pine-needle-carpeted farmland in my bare feet. I can almost smell the sweet fragrances of wisteria, honeysuckle, and crabapple floating through the air as my heart transports me back to that simpler day. I searched for the biggest pine cones I could find. In the springtime, I was delighted when I discovered wild Rooster Violets blooming in obscure places. It thrilled me to take a fistful of those purple beauties to my mom. She'd put them in a small vase on our whatnot shelf.

I remember chasing my purple-dyed pet chicken—a thrilling little kid freebie that came with my new Easter Shoes—compliments of our local Poole's Department store. I'd carefully chosen the tiny purple-dyed chick from a rainbow of colored ones, and long after most of her dye faded away, she'd still let me pick her up.

I grew up eating homegrown watermelons that were cooled in the old refrigerated vat leftover from our dairy farm days. I loved homemade ice cream—one of the benefits of milking our dairy cows. It was understood that I was the one to sit on top of our old manual ice cream freezer as it reached its hard-to-crank stage—old newspapers separated me from my icy seat.

It was an innocent time when apple was strictly a fruit, children were the remotes for black and white TVs, and the local radio stations played a mixture of country, Gospel, and pop phonograph records.

Ma' Bell party lines and eavesdropping neighbors were the norm, and long distance was too expensive to use. Handwritten letters were mailed often to keep in touch, and supper was always served with sweet tea and cornbread. Fast food was leftovers warmed quickly on the gas stove in a day when lunch was called dinner.

It was a wonderful time and place for a starry-eyed, brown-headed girl to grow up. In those sheltered years of my childhood, I could've never imagined the heartaches, disappointments, and grief that awaited me.

I met my Prince Charming when I was eighteen, and by my twenty-first birthday, he'd whisked me away to a land called Oklahoma. Pine cones and Rooster Violets were few and far between, but life seemed wonderful, and loss and pain were something that happened to other people—until they happened to me.

When I was twenty-six, my dad was diagnosed with a brain tumor. I flew back and forth to Mississippi and helped care for him as cancer took his life. Less than two years later, our newborn daughter suffered major brain damage when she was only eight days old, and overnight, with no medical training or preparation, I embarked on a long-term journey of caring for our precious critical care child.

When I was forty-nine, my oldest brother died suddenly of a heart attack, and six months later, my sister was diagnosed with a reoccurrence of melanoma. I spent my fiftieth birthday beside her hospital bed in Alabama as she lay dying. Her death occurred exactly twelve days from the first-year anniversary of my brother's death.

As I reeled from those losses, my Prince Charming, my beloved of nearly thirty-three years, was diagnosed with melanoma also. That was a triple-sucker punch to the stomach. At one point, my husband and my daughter were both on hospice. I could hardly believe it, and by the time I was fifty-two, I wore the unwanted title of widow.

My daughter died three years later, and my son and I buried her beside her daddy. Three months after that, my mom suffered a stroke, but thankfully she survived. Eight years after Mike died, I was blessed to remarry. Two years later, my new sweetheart faced a failed heart surgery, which launched us into a new battle—eating to live—because no medical solution was available for his situation.

How About You?

When I was skipping barefoot through those hills of Mississippi, I couldn't have imagined the hardships I would later face. I thought I'd meet my Prince Charming, and we'd live happily ever after and grow old together, but then life blindsided me. It seemed to sucker-punch me again and again. You may feel that way as well—but in my journey, I learned that nothing, nothing ever blindsides God. He will take the tragedies in our lives and turn them into triumphs when we keep our focus on Him.

Have you experienced your own hard seasons, or are you in the midst of one right now? If I could sit beside you and share a cup of coffee, I'd tell you this: whatever you are going through, no matter how painful and difficult it is, He sees your hard place and your hurt, He cares about you, and He's walking beside you. He is your living hope and your strength through it all, and when you choose to turn over all those broken and painful pieces, He'll work them to your good and bring forth purpose in your pain.

"You keep track of all my sorrows. You have collected all my tears in your bottle. You have recorded each one in your book" (Psalm 56:8, NLT).

My Childhood

I grew up as the baby girl in a family of six—one older sister and two older brothers. I used to hate to be introduced as the "baby," but at seventy, I rather relish it now.

My sister, Lynda, played the piano beautifully, and when I was knee-high, she'd stand me on the piano bench right beside her as she banged out various tunes on our old upright piano.

Our two-bedroom white-frame house, built by my dad and granddad in the 1930s, was on a foundation with a crawl space underneath. Lynda's piano playing rattled the windows and shook the floors and walls. Elvis Presley tunes, like Jail House Rock, had that whole house rocking, and I loved it.

My mom—not so much—particularly if she was in the kitchen cooking supper. That old piano sat against the wall—a wall shared by the kitchen. I'm sure that stove would dance a bit as well as the pots and pans…thus why my mom wasn't quite as excited about Lynda and me doing our duets.

Lynda taught me the words of her songs as I sang along with her. I especially remember singing songs like "This Little Light of Mine," "I'm Gonna' Let it Shine," and "Let the Sunshine In," as well as "Jesus Loves the Little Children," and I eventually learned to pick out "At the Cross" by myself on that same old piano. Such fun memories, memories that I now see as strong foundations of His grace, positioned into my life because seventy years later, I still have the words of most of those hymns memorized.

Since I was a late-in-life child, my sister, Lynda, and two brothers, Jerry and Wayne, were gone from home by the time I was eight and a half. I missed singing with my sister, but I'd go down the hill from our front porch to what we called the hollow, and I vividly remember standing on the bank by myself belting out "Do Lord, Oh Do Lord, Do Remember Me," as well as, "Jesus Loves Me," and a number of other songs I loved.

My mom was a homemaker, and my dad was a math teacher at the city school, as well as a farmer. We spent our summers gathering the fresh veggies that grew from the seeds my dad planted in the spring. By summer's end, we'd canned green beans, pickled dozens of jars of my mom's wonderful bread-and-butter pickles, and had frozen several dozen bags of creamed corn.

We usually shelled, bagged, and froze a bumper crop of purple hulled black-eyed peas too. My thumbs stayed purple half the summer because daddy and I were the designated shellers. Pears and peaches were a favorite to freeze as well. By July, our big chest-type freezer was filled. As you can imagine, our summers were long and very busy, and I only saw my girlfriends at church on Sunday.

Once school started, the winter months were spent studying and helping my dad hay the cows. Haying the cows involved my dad loading the old trailer with a few bales of hay and my climbing into the truck cab or onto the tractor as I jammed in the clutch and pulled that two-wheel trailer. (I'd learned to drive when I was nine years old, as many farm kids did.) My dad would stand on the back of that trailer and toss the hay bales into the field as the excited cattle bellowed after us. More than once, I bounced my dad off that trailer. He jokingly told me one day that he thought I'd pulled him through every gopher hole in the field. Needless to say, my life was certainly quite different from many of my city friends.

I was raised in the same beautiful antebellum-styled church that my dad and his parents before him were. Many of my family members, including my parents, were baptized in the nearby Graves Creek before the church built the baptistry, where I was later baptized. That church—Improve Baptist—is still a beacon of light today. My nephew (my dad's only Powell grandson) and his sweet wife are members there today. My mom, dad, grandparents, and great-grandparents are buried in the cemetery that sits right beside the church.

Other remembrances include sitting beside my sweet grandma Aby on the front row of the church, sweating through summer revivals (before there was air conditioning), followed by dinner on the grounds after the Sunday morning revival kickoff service. As I fondly reminisce, I can almost smell the fried chicken and taste Mrs. Hazel's luscious three-layered caramel cake that I always tried to grab a piece of.

And I distinctly remember one morning in my Sunday school class as my favorite SS teacher, Mrs. Ruth Cox, led us in singing "Jesus Loves Me." I'd been singing Jesus Sloves Me and had no idea what that meant! But that morning, when I was four or five, I really heard the words and realized they said "Jesus." "Loves." "Me!" It felt like a warm hug to my heart.

It wasn't until I was eleven that I invited Christ into my heart, though. On the last night of one of those summer revivals, seated midway back in the church pew, I sweated from the sweltering Mississippi heat as well as the conviction that tugged at my heart. The old ceiling fan churned that humid air as the choir sang "Softly and Tenderly

Jesus is Calling." It was then that I heard His still small voice speak, "Come home, child."

Timidly, I walked to the front of the sanctuary and bowed my head, asked His forgiveness, and invited Him into my heart. I knew that my life would never be the same. In fact, I wrote in my childhood diary (which is now very much an antique) these words, "Today is the most important day of my life because I invited Jesus to be my Lord and Savior."

And as time went by, I did what most teenage girls did in the sixties. I went to school, had crushes on boys, rolled my hair, sat under the new-fangled-bonnet-hair dryer, and went to church to visit God.

Unfortunately, I didn't think much about God or talk to Him unless I was at church or I had something troubling me. I'd read the Ten Commandments and was pretty certain I kept them. I knew I'd spend eternity with Him.

I must admit I was more of a rule-keeper and a Goody Two-shoes than a grace-filled child of God. I didn't understand that I could daily enjoy a sweet personal relationship with Him. Instead, I adhered to my unwritten list of dos and don'ts. I mistakenly thought the Christian life was all about performance. I made good grades, never smoked, drank, or cussed, but I also never felt concerned about whether my classmates knew Christ or not because I was too busy being good and performing. After all, I knew Him, my family knew Him, and so did my best friend.

I'd soon learn that wherever I was, whatever I faced—God would meet me there and teach me about His grace and love and what making Him Lord of my life really looked like.

At age eighteen, I sat on my front porch in our old swing in the cool of the day. I'd been given a pocket-sized pamphlet by a young missionary who'd visited our church. I held it, and I still remember flipping to the back to see who wrote it...it was compliments of Campus Crusade for Christ.

As I read it, once again, my Heavenly Father spoke to my heart. He used that little booklet mightily—right where I was—on my front porch—in that swing! It was then that I realized He wanted a daily personal relationship with me—one where I let Him guide my actions and my thoughts—one where He was in control, not me. And from that day forward, I learned that His grace would meet me faithfully time and again—right where I was—to teach me and encourage me.

I cried and asked Him to help me walk closer to Him, and I also prayed that He'd send me a husband.

Wedding Bells

That summer of 1969, a handsome young man, Michael Whitley—from Oklahoma—visited my small church. When he first walked in, I wondered, "Lord, could this be the one I've prayed for?"

A secretary from Mike's office realized how lonely he must be and graciously invited that Catholic boy to our Baptist church to meet our young people. It seems like yesterday that we were introduced on the front lawn of my church. He shared that he was working for Gulf Oil in a work/study program between his junior and senior years at Oklahoma State University.

I couldn't help but notice that he had the most beautiful grey-blue eyes and the longest black eyelashes. His black hair, olive complexion, and easy laugh captivated this eighteen-year-old girl. I was quite smitten, can you tell?

Back at home, I looked up Oklahoma in the encyclopedia (the google of the sixties and seventies) because I had no idea where it was located. (I regret that geography was never one of my favorite subjects.) I never dreamed when I glimpsed Oklahoma on that map that I'd spend most of the rest of my life where the wind comes sweeping down the plain.

Mike continued to visit our church, and by July, he mustered up enough courage to ask me for a date. That first date remains forever etched in my memories, even though it occurred over fifty-two years ago. We drove to Hattiesburg in his old white clunker of a car, we ate at a small local pizza place called Pasquale's, and we laughed and talked the whole time. After that, we went to the movie and watched True Grit with John Wayne, and we talked all the way back home. I remember telling him, "I really like you," and I did. We dated the rest of the summer. This country girl taught that city boy a lot about farm life. Mike learned how to saddle our old gray mare. She was my brother Wayne's horse and that summer was hanging out at our house for some reason. She looked like she was ready for the glue factory, and she was stubborn and had an attitude. Many times, as we rode on the old harnessed horse, she'd stop to eat blackberries along the fence line—without our permission. Eventually, she'd meander where else she wanted to go as we held on and continued to ride and visit. It was a fun and sweet time in our lives…a time to get to know each other.

When Mike returned to Oklahoma in the fall, we continued to date via occasional phone calls (long distance was very expensive back then) and, of course, letters. He returned on a Grey Hound Bus (he found it was cheaper than putting gas in his old car) and spent Thanksgiving with my family, and then he drove down in his clunker for his spring break. I wasn't off for break until the next week, so a friend of mine found him a bed at the Hattiesburg Y for his nights, and he visited with me all week, even sitting in on some of my classes at USM.

The following summer, Gulf Oil offered him a job working one week offshore in Louisiana, and we found him a room in a private home in our town to rent during his week off. During one of those weeks off, we drove to Oklahoma, so I could meet his dad and grandmother, and we were married on December 22, 1970—only three days after he graduated from Oklahoma State. We pledged our vows in the little church where we'd met, and a whole new chapter in our lives began.

God's Grace Keeping Pace

I see beautiful glimpses of God's grace throughout my growing-up years. He is with each of us and for each of us each step of the way. He knows our end from the beginning, so He equips us with what we'll need to navigate our days. Let's remember to steadily look for His graces because He never leaves our side.

Chapter 2
THERE'S A SWEET, SWEET SPIRIT

"So do not fear, for I am with you; do not be dismayed, for I am your God. I will strengthen you and help you; I will uphold you with my righteous right hand" (Isaiah 41:10. NIV).

I'd been called by many titles growing up: daughter, baby sister, granddaughter, friend, student, and Christian—to name a few, but I loved adding my new title of Mrs. Whitley. Mike and I settled into married life in a small three-room furnished cottage that I'd located by word of mouth. Our rent was a whopping eighty-five dollars a month, and we entered married life with three hundred and fifty dollars to our name. My parents allowed us to wash our clothes on weekends at their house until we were able to afford our first washing machine. We added two chairs to our little furnished cottage that I'd found hanging on an outbuilding wall on the farm. I refinished them, and they still sit in our home today. We carefully counted our pennies and gradually bought used furniture as we saved monthly for our first home.

We were blessed to live in Mississippi for one and a half years after we married. That was a good thing because I'd never been away from home longer than five days. Even when I was in college, my best friend, Celia, and I left on Monday mornings in her '53 Chevy for our forty-minute drive to USM, and we returned on Friday evenings.

Mike was eventually offered a job in Oklahoma, and we moved in the fall of 1972. On the day before we left, my second pregnancy test finally came back positive. I'd thrown up for three months at the sight of raw meat or the smell of food cooking. When my first pregnancy test came back negative, I was concerned. If I wasn't pregnant, I thought I might be dying of some dread disease, so I was excited when the second test identified my symptoms.

Armed with the exciting news that by spring, we'd be parents, we left for Oklahoma with our 1970 Monte Carlo packed to the brim. As we drove down the long-graveled lane that led away from the only home I'd ever known, I cried. Would I ever live in Mississippi again?

The more miles Mike and I put behind us, the more I missed those tall pines and my sweet parents. But the beautiful biblical words of Ruth 1:16b–17a (NIV) sum it up: "Where you go I will go, and where you stay I will stay. Your people will be my people and your God my God. Where you die, I will die, and there I will be buried."

I gladly went, but I didn't realize how hard that change would initially be. I soon learned that homesickness was real. I didn't realize then that those flat plains of Oklahoma would become my "forever home."

My mom would meet the movers as soon as we found a place to live. They'd load our meager household goods and drive them to our new address in Pauls Valley, Oklahoma. Our first two weeks were spent in a hotel as we hunted for that new address. I slept with saltine crackers beside the bed and munched them off and on all night long for my persistent waves of nausea and homesickness. We had indeed embarked on another new chapter in our lives, and ironically, our new address was 104 Memory Lane.

Before the homesickness could fade, the morning sickness went away because, in April, we were blessed by the birth of a beautiful, healthy baby boy, Benjamin Michael. He weighed eight pounds and thirteen ounces, and the new title of mom made me so happy. I wrote letters to my parents weekly, telling them all about baby Ben as all my energy went into caring for my precious family.

I had very little time for God. Of course, I continued to meet Him every Sunday at church, and I read an occasional devotional for good measure. Without realizing it, I'd resumed my previous role of being good and following my list of dos and don'ts. A form of religion once again replaced my daily fellowship with God. I, again, assumed that was all He desired and all I needed.

In 1974, Mike and I moved from Paul's Valley to Yukon, Oklahoma—a suburb of Oklahoma City—when Mike was offered yet another new job. We settled in, and I learned to navigate the more congested highways of Oklahoma City. We found a church, made new friends, and life was good.

1975 Change of Plans

The holidays were upon us, and I was more excited than usual because it'd be the first Christmas that I'd spent in Mississippi since I'd become a mom. My to-do list was long, and one by one, I'd checked off the things jotted on it. Among the important things on that list was to make a batch of peanut brittle. That was one of my dad's favorites. I'd just failed at that attempt when the telephone rang, and my day went sour in an instant.

The caller was my brother, Jerry. "Pam, I've got bad news. Daddy has been diagnosed with a brain tumor, and it doesn't look good.

They've already scheduled brain surgery."

Surely this couldn't be true. My dad had always been healthy. He'd retired two years earlier at age sixty-two to enjoy the farm. He'd always taken good care of himself. Besides that, his parents had lived to their late eighties.

Several weeks earlier, Mike and I had sent my mom and dad plane tickets so they could fly up the week before Christmas, and we'd planned to drive back to Mississippi together—in time to spend Christmas on the farm. I had carefully planned it all and looked so forward to their Oklahoma visit, followed by Christmas on the farm.

My dad taught wiring on B-52 bombers at Keesler AFB during the war, but he'd never ridden on a plane. I wanted to make certain that he had that opportunity. My grandpa Powell had died the year before, and we still grieved his absence. The last time I'd visited with him, he'd commented that he had one regret in life—he'd never gotten to fly on an airplane. I wasn't able to change that for my granddad, but I could give that opportunity to my own dad. So those tickets were to be my dad and mom's Christmas present from us—a plane flight to Oklahoma.

I hung up the phone with a broken heart, and I canceled my folks' flight as I threw my important to-do list in the trash. The earliest airline ticket to Mississippi that I could afford put my arrival there on the day of my dad's surgery.

So, December 17, 1975, dawned with me and two-year-old Ben boarding a plane for Mississippi. Mike would drive down as soon as his vacation started. Fortunately, Ben and I were able to fly into Jackson, and when we arrived, we weren't far from the hospital where my dad was. The pastor from my mother and daddy's church picked us up.

When I arrived at the hospital, my dad was already in surgery. Sadly, I'd soon learn that I'd never have another conversation with him because the procedure left him partially paralyzed on one side and, for the most part, unable to speak. The surgery revealed that the malignant tumor had put out fingers into the brain at the base of his skull, and the doctors were unable to remove it all. Their attempt left him with some brain damage. His long-term outlook, unfortunately, was poor.

In all my twenty-five years, I'd never faced such a crisis, and I was ill-equipped for the battle. Fear and worry became my constant companions as I grieved the heartache my mom and dad were enduring.

For six months, with Ben on one hip and a diaper bag and toys slung across my shoulder, I flew back and forth to Mississippi, alternating caregiving duties with my sister, Lynda, who lived in Alabama. I'd stay three to four weeks and then swap with Lynda as she took a turn. My brothers helped as well. It was such a difficult time for all of our family. While I was in Mississippi, I worried about Mike, who was alone in Oklahoma, and when I was in Oklahoma, I worried about my mom and dad's struggle in Mississippi. I developed colitis, and my health deteriorated as worry and fear totally consumed me. My dad's country doctor gave me vitamin B12 injections weekly while I was in Mississippi to help with my stamina.

In spite of my lack of trust, God was so faithful. He'd given me a wonderful new Christian friend in Yukon—Ginger. She'd nurse me back to health physically and spiritually each time I returned to Oklahoma.

One such day occurred on one of my return trips to Oklahoma.

The doorbell rang, and there stood Ginger with a fresh-baked loaf of homemade sourdough bread in one hand and a copy of *The Hiding Place* (by Corrie ten Boom) in the other.

Having no time to read, I left the book in Oklahoma as I made yet another trek to Mississippi. The day I arrived, my aunt, Mammie Lou, brought me a copy of a book—guess what it was—*The Hiding Place*. I decided God definitely wanted me to read that book.

Sitting at the foot of my dad's hospital bed, feeling very sorry for him and very sorry for myself, I devoured that book—page after page.

Corrie and her family hid many Jewish people from the Nazis in a secret room in their home. As the danger escalated, she asked her dad this question.

"Father, if we're caught and sent to a concentration camp, how will we be able to bear it?"

His wise answer was, "Corrie, when we ride the train, when does the conductor give us our ticket?"

"When we board the train."

"Corrie, that is exactly how it is with God's grace; He grants it when you board the train—when you need it most."

This was such a great tool of hope for me that day—the absolute knowledge that God would always meet me with His grace when I needed it the most. That was the first life tool of hope I grabbed from Corrie's story. It would serve me well for the rest of my life.

The next truth that I pocketed in my sad state of self-pity was one that has served me lifelong as well. Corrie's sister Betsy was the spiritually mature one, always praising God daily, no matter what they faced. In fact, as they sat in their flea-ridden barracks of the concentration camp, Corrie resented how positive Betsy was about everything and said tauntingly to her, "I bet you think we should praise God for all of these fleas!"

To which Betsy happily chirped, "Well, yes! As a matter of fact, I'm going to praise Him for these fleas right now," and Betsy praised Him, right then and there!

Corrie thought her sister was nuts as Betsy bowed her head in the middle of their dirty and cold barracks—and gave thanks to God for all things, including those fleas. Later they'd find out why women in their barracks weren't violated or bothered by the guards as other women in other barracks were—those fleas were their protection. Not only that, but they realized the reason they could teach the women freely about Christ and give them hope in their desolate place—was those fleas!

As I read those pages of Corrie's pain, I realized that my Heavenly Father loved me just the same. He wasn't a respecter of persons, nor had He changed. My focus was totally turned inward to my pain and my folk's pain—I'd not looked to God for strength. Instead, I'd cried, I'd begged, I'd grumbled, and I'd complained to God. All along, though, He'd wanted to meet my needs in the midst of my storm, just as He'd met Corrie's and Betsy's. I knelt and prayed at the foot of my dad's hospital bed that day and confessed my lack of faith and trust. I determined I'd learn to praise Him too—in all things.

Weak and scared, I began my new journey of learning how to trust God and His Word in my storms. I had much to relearn because my independent young self was not accustomed to relying on God daily. "You're blessed when you're at the end of your rope. With less of you there is more of God and his rule" (Matthew 5:3, MSG).

As I read His scripture daily and learned to praise Him in all things, my focus turned to Him rather than my circumstances. I threw the prescription valium into the trash because the colitis went away when I'd finally lay my burdens at His feet. I learned a wonderful lesson too; while I couldn't trace God's hand, I could/can always, always trust His heart.

I asked God to allow me to be in Mississippi when my dad died. I flew back on May 7, 1976, because we were told my precious dad was at death's door. I'd not seen him in five weeks. When I arrived late that day, my brother, Jerry, tried to prepare me for the sight I would witness upon entering my daddy's room.

Several men from our church kept vigil in the room beside my brother. I gasped when I saw Daddy because he had deteriorated a great deal in the last five weeks. My strong daddy probably now weighed ninety pounds or less, and his body was a shell of the man he'd once been. It broke me. But my sweet Lord chose that moment to bless me beyond what I could've ever imagined. As I walked to where he lay, I heard in my heart an orchestra playing right beside my dad's bed, and I heard a beautiful angelic choir singing softly a song I knew well:

>There's a Sweet, Sweet Spirit in this Place:
>And I know that it's the spirit of the Lord
>Without a doubt we'll know
>That he has been revived
>When he shall leave this place
>
>*"Sweet, Sweet Spirit"*
>Copyright © 1962 Manna Music (ASCAP)

I sang that song almost every week at my church, but the lyrics were, we have been revived, when we shall leave this place. What I heard distinctly in that moment was, *he has been revived when he shall leave this place*. I wept because I felt God, in His grace, was reaching out in an amazing way to walk me through this hard loss. I was filled with God's peace as I felt His presence.

Another sweet thing occurred that day as well. My sister, Lynda, had a C-section on Friday, April 23. Her Alabama home was five hours away, and her doctor would not permit her to travel home to Mississippi until baby Nicole was two weeks old. Nicole was two weeks and one day old on May 8 when our dad went home. My sister arrived a few hours before he graduated from his dying body to his heavenly home! Our God is such an Awesome and Personal God!

The Rest of the Story of His Grace Keeping Pace

When my dad retired from his lifelong career as a public-school teacher, his first retirement project was to add an extra bedroom and bathroom to their farmhouse. He'd already cut down several trees and had them milled into lumber as he prepared to add the new addition. A few weeks before his diagnosis, Daddy had complained about numbness in his right hand. My mom also observed that he'd dropped his fork several times as he ate, and she'd mentioned that to me. I assured her that he'd probably strained a muscle or a nerve with all the heavy lifting and hard work he was doing.

I was so certain that was the culprit of his symptoms that I'd not allowed much thought of any other possibility. That is, until my brother's call. I was totally blindsided by the brain tumor diagnosis, and I was equally blindsided that it happened before we had our Oklahoma visit and our special Christmas on the farm.

"Lord," I sobbed, "I don't understand. If this had to happen, why couldn't it have been after the holidays? Your timing couldn't be worse. Why couldn't we have had our special Christmas?" What a naive young lady I was!

I'd looked forward to my parents flying to Oklahoma and then our return trip to Mississippi, and my finite focus was totally on my own plan. I was disappointed in God because He'd not allowed me to have that well-crafted plan of mine and that special Christmas I had planned.

Now, instead of their visit to Oklahoma, I was flying to Mississippi for my dad's brain surgery! As the plane descended in Mississippi, I caught a glimpse of the lush green pines of home, and I held Ben tightly as grief washed over me and tears streamed down my face.

Again, I begged, "God, please let Daddy be okay! Let Ben grow up knowing him."

To make matters worse, the Jackson hospital was almost two hours from my parent's home. It was too far to drive back and forth, so my sister and brothers, who were already there, had rented motel rooms the first night so we'd be near my dad. The extra cost strained all of our budgets.

Some Christmas, Lord, I thought angrily. Again, the naive young woman that I was, I was clueless as far as my faith went, and I was only focused on my own plan.

On the second day of my dad's hospital stay, a legislator from our hometown came by the hospital to check on us. He was a family friend who had grown up on the farm next to ours. After our visit, as he prepared to leave, Mr. Emerson pulled a key from his pocket and handed it to us.

"The legislature is officially on Christmas break, and my two roommates and I are headed home today. Our apartment is yours through the rest of December. It's not far from the hospital."

We checked out of our motel rooms and located the apartment. Each of the three bedrooms had a private bath; the apartment was completely furnished and had its own washer and dryer. When my sister and I weren't at the hospital, we shopped for Christmas presents. We all took turns staying with my dad, and we shared many sweet times together, not only at the hospital but also in our borrowed home. That apartment was a double blessing too because my sister was pregnant and not feeling well.

On Christmas Eve, my dad was dismissed, and we were able to take him home. When we arrived back on the farm, someone had brought us a fresh-cut pine tree. My sister and I pulled out my mom and dad's old decorations, and she and I decorated the tree that night. Neighbors and friends had filled the house with wonderful Southern food. We had a sad but very blessed Christmas after all.

Today as I recall how I railed at God about His timing, I am so humbled. My sister and her husband lived out of state and were school teachers also. They were on Christmas break. My husband and I had scheduled our vacation time because of our planned trip. At no other time of the year would the apartment have been available, nor would we all have had vacation time. God's grace had provided beautifully for each of us.

It's been forty-seven years since that long-ago Christmas, but the memories are etched in my heart forever. It was my dad's last Christmas, but he had all of his kids gathered around him as we drew close to God and to each other. And I learned that while unexpected things may blindside us, they never blindside God. His timing is perfect. His grace truly does keep pace with whatever we face.

After my dad's death, our life returned to a new normal. Mike and I bought a new home in Oklahoma City, one that had a mother-in-law suite, because we wanted my newly widowed mom to have her own private area when she came to visit. We attempted to leave the pain behind. Within a few months, we were expecting our second child, and once again, I slept with saltine crackers by the bed. We had no idea that we stood at the threshold of a cold, dark, and deep valley.

God's Grace Keeping Pace

God meets us each step of the way as we live our lives. Jesus, Himself said in John 16:33 (KJV), "These things I have spoken unto you, that in me ye might have peace. In the world ye shall have tribulation: but be of good cheer; I have overcome the world." When life blindsides us, we have His Manufacture's Handbook, the Bible, to guide us through it all. He is faithful.

Chapter 3
GREAT IS THY FAITHFULNESS

> The steadfast love of the Lord never ceases;
> his mercies never come to an end;
> they are new every morning;
> great is your faithfulness.
> "The Lord is my portion," says my soul,
> "therefore I will hope in him."
>
> Lamentations 3:22–24 (ESV)

The due date of our second baby was December 22, 1977. I was excited because that would be our eighth wedding anniversary, as well as my dad's birthday. We still grieved his loss greatly. What a special blessing it would be if this baby was born on that doubly special date. Christmas was the next potential special date, followed by New Year's.

But the twenty-second came and went, and so did Christmas. My five-foot-two frame now waddled, and my tummy was so large I couldn't see my feet. I was more than ready to meet our baby.

In 1977, although ultrasound imaging had been invented, it wasn't used other than for a crisis situation, so we didn't know our baby's gender. In that day, the big gender reveal was literally on the day the baby was born. I'd decorated the nursery in neutral colors of green and yellow as we awaited our little one's arrival.

Mike teased about needing a tax write-off for 1977 as he hoped for a December birth. I hoped for a December birth, too, but because of those swollen feet and my huge out-in-front tummy that preceded me as I waddled into a room. Four-year-old brother, Ben, just wanted a brother or sister to play with, and the sooner, the better.

December 31 came, and since there'd been no birth, we invited friends over for a simple New Year's Eve dinner. Their two sons and Ben played as we adults chatted around the crackling wood fire. At about 10:00 p.m., my tummy felt strange, and soon, I recognized that strange feeling as labor pains. We were so excited. Our baby was getting ready to be born. Maybe Mike would get his tax write-off after all? We'd soon find out.

We grabbed my overnight bag and headed to the hospital. Our sweet Ben was born in 1973 in Pauls Valley, Oklahoma, and we'd since moved to Oklahoma City. The hospital we chose for this birth was a fifteen-minute drive from our home and was fairly new, having been built in 1974. It was in a yet-to-be-built-up area of town, and on a New Year's Eve, it was not a happening place. The bored staff were very excited to see us.

By the time we arrived and filled out the necessary paperwork, it was eleven thirty, and my labor pains were getting closer and closer together. I was hurriedly prepped for the delivery room as they helped me change into a hospital gown and climb onto a cold metal table. They told me to sit as straight as I could so they could give me a spinal block.

It's not the discomfort of the injection that I remember, but rather the remarks the anesthesiologist made to the nurse and to me, "Look how crooked her spine is!"

He said to me, "Have you ever been diagnosed with scoliosis?"

At that moment, I didn't care how my back looked, and I wanted to say, "Did you know it's rude to talk behind someone's back?" As I sat awkwardly leaning forward, crossed-legged, balancing my bulging tummy on that icy table, I just wanted to see my baby—and my feet.

In 1978, that hospital still didn't allow dads into the delivery room. So, Mike kissed me goodbye and waited in the new-to-be-fathers waiting area alone. My mom was sent to yet another waiting room, and she, too, was the only one there. As they whisked me through the delivery room doors, one of the nurses commented to the others, "Guys, we could have the first baby of '78."

Later I heard them say from my awkward prone position, "It's midnight!" and I knew Mike wouldn't be getting his little tax write-off! Ticktock, ticktock.

Another nurse called the nurses' station from the delivery room and asked them to check with the major hospitals in Oklahoma City to see if a baby had been born yet in '78. They were excited to relay back to the delivery room that there hadn't been.

Someone said eagerly, "You know, we had the first baby last year in OKC, and I think we may do it again this year." And just like that, I had a cheering squad encouraging me to push, mama, push. Believe me, I was already doing my part.

I think the older doctor tired of their delivery room antics and decided he'd put an end to their little pep rally, "I've delivered babies as early as 12:05 on January 1, and I've never delivered a New Year's baby. This will not be the first baby of the year."

And when he delivered our baby at 12:54, the nurses quickly checked one more time and cheered because our baby was indeed the first baby born in 1978 in Oklahoma City, weighing in at seven pounds and eleven ounces. As they celebrated being first in OKC, I rejoiced that I was holding an adorable and beautiful little dark-headed, bright-eyed baby girl. She was one of 335,996 babies born on that January 1 day in the United States. I don't think any one of them was more welcomed than our little beauty.

People often ask me whether there was a prize for having that first baby of the year in Oklahoma City. Well, yes and no. My reward was a 7:00-a.m. loud rap on my hospital-room door. It was flung open as a nurse ushered in two cameramen, one from Channel 4 and one from Channel 5, and a news anchor, as well as a newspaperman. Mike and I often watched Linda Cavanaugh, the news anchor, on TV, and it was a treat to meet her. They were all eager to meet and take pictures of our little one—after all, she was Oklahoma City's newest little citizen.

My first thought as they entered our room was, Oh my; I can't imagine what I must look like! I begged the nurse for a hairbrush and mirror before those shutters snapped. Thankfully, she quickly opened the over-the-bed tray so I could peek at myself in the small mirror that flipped up. What I saw was one tired mama, sporting dark circles under her eyes, enhanced by her bob with bangs that stuck straight up in the air. Oh my. I used the only resource I had in those few seconds—my fingertips and my spit—as I tried to make those unruly bangs lay down.

I'd also been told to lay flat for twenty-four hours following the spinal injection, but the bed was quickly rolled upright for the photo-shoot as our sweet baby was placed in my arms. Cameras clicked as

Janice Marie Whitley's first pictures were taken, and Mike and I and Jan were on TV by evening and in the newspaper the next morning.

Countless people clipped that newspaper picture and mailed it to us, congratulating us on our new baby. The newspaper guy had Mike's name wrong and introduced the parents of the New Year's baby as Mr. and Mrs. George Whitley. He, the newspaper guy, probably had celebrated a bit too much on New Year's Eve, but anyone who knew us recognized us. Little did we know that those pictures would be among the few ever taken of our normal little girl—pictures taken before the trauma of January 8.

The Heart Break

January 8, 1978, ensued with a frantic 2:00 a.m. drive to the ER where Jan had been born only the week before. Earlier that Saturday morning, I'd thought Jan's breathing was a little fast. Concerned, I grabbed my trusted old baby book and searched for information on infant breathing patterns. (Neither Google nor the internet had been invented back then.) The baby book said that sometimes new parents become alarmed because they think their newborn is breathing too rapidly, but newborns breathe at a faster rate. I assumed that I was being an overprotective new mom.

After all, I'd been sick with a virus the night before, and I'd suffered a horrible side effect from that spinal block. My not lying flat for twenty-four hours following that injection had left me with a week of terrible migraines. I thought my fatigue and migraine were affecting my judgment, and I was overreacting.

Night came. Mike put Ben to bed and called it a night himself. Even though Jan was sleeping soundly, I picked her up and walked back and forth in the den cradling her in my arms. The more I held her and walked, the more my apprehension grew. My mom stayed up with me, sharing my concern. She'd come from Mississippi to spend Christmas with us and to welcome her new grandbaby.

"Mother, I have this uneasy feeling that something is wrong with Jan. I don't know what to do."

I decided to call the hospital nursery where she'd been born the week before. I was fortunate enough to talk with one of the sweet cheerleading nurses, and she remembered us well. I shared my concerns, and she asked a few questions and suggested that I continue to watch her carefully and call the doctor if there were more symptoms.

Sometime after midnight, as I still walked the floor holding Jan, I pulled off her booties. Her feet were purple. Being the innocent young woman I was, I thought her booties were too tight. But within minutes, purple splotches appeared on Jan's legs. A lump rose in my throat, and my heart pounded. I knew something was terribly wrong.

Because of the many people who had visited our home over the past two days, I told myself Jan had picked up a weird virus. I woke Mike and called our doctor as we rushed Jan to the same hospital where she'd been born. We made the drive in less than fifteen minutes in spite of icy roads. Mike was scared. He'd seen the purple feet, and at one point, I asked him to slow down because the roads were so treacherous, and we were going very fast. By the time we walked into the emergency room, Jan's once rosy face was blue, and upon examination, the emergency room doctor said he detected a heart murmur.

We'd just brought her home from the hospital three days before. Surely this couldn't be true! A heart specialist was called from Children's Hospital, and for the first time, I realized this was much more than a virus. Mike and I were sent to a private area to await the doctor's arrival.

The specialist arrived around 4:00 a.m. After examining Jan, he took us into a small room and pulled up a chair. He sat down slowly as if allowing himself extra seconds to choose his words carefully. Looking into our eyes, he told us that our sweet Jan was in critical condition.

"In order for us to find out what type of heart problem your daughter has, we have to transfer her to Children's Hospital immediately. At this point, I know that she has one of four types of heart defects, and one of those isn't repairable. We'll do a heart catheterization first, and it'll show us what we're dealing with, but I'll be honest with you, Jan is very weak. I don't know if she can survive the catheterization. I'm so sorry, but her chances of living are slim."

We stared at him in shock and disbelief. She'd been rated a 9 on the Apgar scale that determines the health of a newborn—only eight days before. How could this be?

Jan would be transferred to Children's Hospital by ambulance. Since we wouldn't be permitted to ride with her, we were allowed to kiss her goodbye. Walking into her room, I felt dazed and overwhelmed. Jan was in an incubator, and with an oxygen mask, she still struggled for each breath. Her beautiful pink complexion was now dusky gray. It seemed a part of me was being destroyed, and I could only stand by helplessly and do nothing. Never had my arms felt so empty and my heart so crushed.

I knew that my mother was probably still awake, waiting to hear the diagnosis. I couldn't bear to tell her such devastating news over the phone. She was in her sixties, and the loss of my dad had been so hard on her. Even though it was still dark outside, I located a pay phone and called my dear friend, Judith, who lived a few blocks from our home. She and her husband were the ones who'd spent New Year's Eve with us, and they'd been at the hospital New Year's morning when Jan was born. While Judith threw on her clothes, I called my mom and told her Judith was on her way and would explain what was going on.

Mike and I took one last look at our chubby-cheeked little girl as we each wondered if this was our final goodbye. Our hearts had never been so broken. In that long-ago day before cell phones or google maps, they'd given us verbal directions to Children's Hospital, so with those instructions fresh in our minds, we rushed out into the icy morning. The drive to Children's seemed to take forever as the blowing snow glistened in the headlights of our car, and the Oklahoma wind whipped our vehicle. We drove cautiously but also as fast as we dared. The nurses had advised us not to follow the ambulance as they cried while we said our goodbyes.

Stunned by the dire diagnosis, we hadn't understood that an ambulance had to come from Children's to pick up Jan, so we arrived several minutes ahead of her. When her arrival was delayed, we thought she'd died en route. We were so distraught.

While Mike filled out the hospital forms, I laid my head on the staff's desk as my head pounded with pain. I couldn't believe yet another tragedy was occurring. It had been less than two years since my dad's death. How I longed to go back to those days before pain found its way into my life, a time when I felt sheltered from life's storms, a time before I'd boarded that train that Corrie ten Boom's dad spoke of. Now it seemed like such a long time ago.

God's Grace Keeping Pace

I believe it was by the grace of God that I stayed awake and on high alert that long-ago Saturday night. Jan would have been gone when we awoke the next morning. In God's grace, He always sent people to walk beside us in our storms too. Let's keep looking for those glimpses of His grace.

"'For I know the plans I have for you,' declares the Lord, 'plans to prosper you and not to harm you, plans to give you hope and a future'" (Jeremiah 29:11, NIV).

"I will instruct you and teach you in the way you should go; I will counsel you with my loving eye on you" (Psalm 32:8, NIV).

"And we know that in all things God works for the good of those who love him, who have been called according to his purpose" (Romans 8:28, NIV).

"Humble yourselves therefore under the mighty hand of God, that he may exalt you in due time" (1 Peter 5:6, KJV).

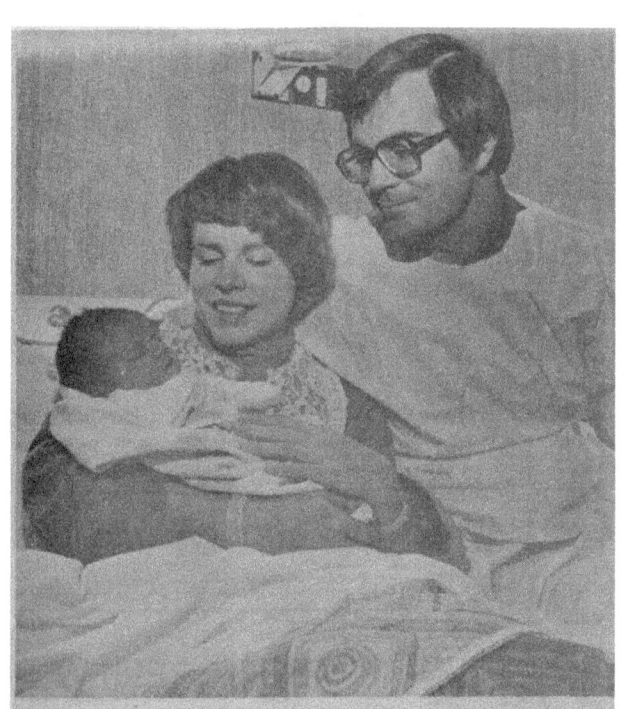

First baby for 1978

Born at 12:54 a.m., Jan. 1, and thus making her the first Fridayland baby for 1978, was Janice Marie Whitley, daughter of Mr. and Mrs. (ichan) Whitley. The Whitleys, who live at 8309 NW 116, have another child, 4-year-old Ben, who was also born on a noteworthy day -- Friday the 13th. (Friday Foto by Steve Sloan)

Chapter 4
SWEETLY BROKEN

"The Lord is close to the brokenhearted and saves those who are crushed in spirit" (Psalm 34:18, NIV).

January 1978

I knew I couldn't go back to the those early sheltered-from-the-storms days, but I longed to. It had been less than two years since my dad's homegoing.

Random thoughts skipped through my pounding head as we waited for the ambulance. *Lord, this baby was supposed to be a fresh start, one that would help us heal from the loss of my dad. Please, let me be having a nightmare. Let me wake up.* But when the nurse came to tell us that the ambulance had arrived, I knew I wasn't dreaming.

As soon as Jan was rolled into the emergency room, a flurry of activity began as she was immediately prepped for the catheterization. Pulling myself together, I knew I must call friends and ask them to pray.

I searched through my coins, and Mike checked his change for dimes as I walked to the pay phones. (Cell phones were practically unheard of back then.) I dialed my friend Ginger's number first. Ironically, exactly one week before, at that same time, I'd called her to share the joy of Jan's birth. How could one week make such a difference?

Next, I dialed our pastor's number. His wife answered. I told her what had happened. "Honey, we'll be right there."

With all the snow and ice on the ground, it was an accomplishment for anyone to drive to Children's. It would have been understandable if no one came, but many people did. Their love and presence brought us strength.

Jan survived the catheterization. We were told that she had a coarctation of the aorta. The doctors explained that it was a birth defect, a narrowing of the aorta. The survival rate for that type of surgery was good.

"If all goes well," they said, "Jan could be well enough to go home in a week."

Finally, finally! Hope.

Our pastor and his wife arrived just before Jan was whisked away for surgery. They prayed for her and us, never leaving our side, not even for our church's Sunday morning service. We were so exhausted mentally and physically that we asked them time and time again to refresh our memories on what the doctors said.

We later learned that a layperson preached to the sparse crowd that had braved the icy roads that morning at our church service so that our pastor, Jack Poe, could stay with us. When church was over, more friends filled the corridor of the hospital. They prayed and waited with us in our waiting room. Our assigned waiting room was a long corridor with a huge sheet of plastic that covered the opening where the new waiting room would soon be. (The hospital was in the middle of remodeling.)

The soon-to-be waiting room didn't have the windows in place yet. As the winter storm raged outside, it blasted again and again against the wall of plastic that served as their temporary windows. The plastic shook and rattled, making the sounds of a flag being whipped in the wind—and the bone-chilling gusts forced their way through the weakest spots in the plastic. I pulled my wool camel-colored coat tightly around my shivering body and pulled the hood up. The icy cold and bleakness that permeated the wall matched what was in my heart and my body.

The minutes clicked by—one hour, two hours, three hours, and finally, after four hours, the surgery was completed. Once again, Jan had survived. However, not without problems. She'd stopped breathing in the midst of the surgery and went without oxygen for a period of fifteen minutes. They'd had to resuscitate her. The doctors hoped that she would be all right. We later learned in those fifteen minutes that our normal little New Year's baby was lost forever.

The day had turned into night before the nurse said, "Mr. and Mrs. Whitley, your baby is out of recovery now. You can see her, but only for ten minutes—no more than two people at a time."

Mike and I hurriedly walked down the long corridor to the ICU area. Not knowing what to expect, we paused momentarily at the double doors as each of us took a deep breath before we walked in. Our hearts were not prepared for what we saw—our panicked baby girl frantically fought the various attachments to her body.

Surely this can't be Jan.

She barely resembled the baby I'd cradled in my arms less than twenty-four hours earlier. A respirator tube was taped to her upper lip, and she moved her head distraughtly from side to side as if trying to escape it. A PICC line jutted from the side of her tiny neck where the IV and medications were given, and a drainage tube protruded out of her lungs. The surgical incision was across her back, and tape covered much of her little body. There were no cell phone cameras back then, but I'm rather glad I have no pictures to preserve that sight that is forever etched in my heart.

One of her tiny legs had begun to turn dark purple and swell where the medication had been pumped rapidly in when she'd stopped breathing. The actual injection site was black—the meds to resuscitate her had literally burned her skin. She couldn't cry or make a sound because of the respirator. More connections were fastened to her chest to monitor her heart rate. We weren't allowed to touch her because it might interfere with the machines. I longed to hold her in my arms and tell her that it would be all right. Would I ever get to hold her again or feed her or hear her cry? Would she be all right?

That night Mike and I drove home on icy roads to spend time with Ben and to try to get some rest. Oklahomans are not accustomed to driving on ice, and as we attempted to turn into our housing addition, our car slid on down the main street. It took us a while to navigate our way back to our own street, but we did eventually make it safely home. I hadn't recovered from the delivery and still was experiencing those intense migraines. Those icy roads only compounded our heartbreak and pain.

Ben was excited to see us. He ran to us, and we hugged him tightly. Poor little guy, he'd been so excited over having a baby sister, and at almost five, he certainly didn't understand what had happened—not that Mike or I did either.

My sweet mom had prepared dinner for us. As we sat down to eat, I looked up and saw Jan's picture on the snack bar—the standard one the hospital took the day Jan was born. Immediately the picture flashed into my mind of how Jan now looked, her little body dependent on all the life support systems, and I collapsed into tears. Was it only a week ago we had celebrated her birth?

God's Grace Keeping Pace

Our pastor and his wife, Jack and Phyllis, were an integral part of pointing us continually toward God and His Word, as were the members of our church. They supported us and poured their love upon us when we needed it the most. Let's keep looking for His glimpses of grace.

Chapter 5
MASTERPIECE

"For we are God's masterpiece. He has created us anew in Christ Jesus, so we can do the good things he planned for us long ago" (Ephesians 2:10, NLT).

The next morning, we awoke early after a very restless night. We once again braved those icy roads and arrived safely. We were hoping and praying that Jan would be better. The doctors told us they'd attempted to take her off the respirator, but she'd been unable to breathe on her own. She was calmer but other than that, she'd not improved. All we could do was wait, watch, and pray.

Tuesday morning, as I walked into the Intensive Care Unit, Jan's eyes rolled back in her head, and her whole body shook. They told us she was having a grand mal seizure. As the day progressed, Jan's entire body swelled. Soon she looked like an inflatable doll that had been expanded to the maximum. She completely stopped fighting the tubes and lapsed into a coma. The only signs of life were the fifteen breaths a minute that the machine automatically breathed for her and the occasional seizure that racked her tiny body. We were told that the swelling was in reaction of the brain being deprived of oxygen during the surgery.

Looking at my precious daughter, now more dead than alive, I cried out, "Lord, where are you? Don't you know what is happening here?"

By Wednesday, Jan had a total of eight doctors involved in her case. They were doing all they knew to do, but Jan's condition continued to worsen.

We were taken to another small room and told, "Mr. and Mrs. Whitley, we've done all we can do for your daughter. There's not a glimmer of hope that she'll live." Those words—not a glimmer of hope—smacked us like an out-of-control freight train. "If for some reason she does live, we believe she'll have major brain damage."

They explained that when the body swells all over, as Jan's had, the brain also swells. The brain can swell only a certain amount before the skull crushes it. They felt the coma had been induced by major areas of the brain being crushed by the skull. Today, they'd remove a portion of the skull to prevent the brain damage, but that was not an option in 1978.

Since she wasn't expected to live, they told me I could now hold her. They pulled a wooden rocker into the minute ICU cubicle and had me sit down. Two nurses gently picked up my lifeless little girl, respirator tube and all, and placed her in my lap. The monitor alarms went off, and I thought she'd died. Her body felt like a plastic doll, not the cuddly little baby I'd last held, but a lifeless doll that took fifteen breaths a minute in response to a machine. My whole body began to shake, and I sobbed uncontrollably in the awful grief of that moment. My dear friend, Judith, stood and wept with me as she wiped my tears and hers too. I wondered if Jan was already gone and those machines were keeping her tiny body alive.

Father, please don't let my baby continue to suffer like this. Please, take her.

Thursday morning, I awoke with overwhelming fear and fatigue. I felt such a heavy burden that I didn't think I could get out of bed. *How long would Jan linger in the coma?* Fear spoke to my mind, enumerating numerous what-ifs. *What if she lives but never comes out of the coma? What if she's in a coma for years? What would we do?* I couldn't hear the Shepherd's voice for listening to fear's loud suggestions. But the Shepherd knew my thoughts and the burden I carried.

Those somber and discouraging thoughts were interrupted by the ringing of the telephone. It was my pastor from Mississippi, the one who picked Ben and me up at the Jackson hospital the day of my dad's surgery. He said, "I just wanted to remind you that God is well able to carry you through this storm."

His words were like a life rope thrown to a drowning person, sent when I needed them the most. I realized that I'd been listening to the voice of fear, not to the Shepherd. That day I chose to trust what He said in His Word rather than follow my emotions. It was a choice I'd have to make many, many more times through the years to turn my eyes on His Word, not my circumstances! "I can do all things through Christ who strengthens me" (Philippians 4:13, NKJV).

We dressed and, once again, went to the hospital. As soon as we arrived, the doctors asked for our consent to run a brain scan on Jan. They told us that if it showed no brain activity, they'd ask our permission to disconnect Jan from life support. While they performed the test, Mike and I, along with his mom and sister Terri, our pastor and his wife, and a friend from church, trudged heavy-heartedly to the hospital chapel to pray. There, in the solitude and privacy of the small chapel, I contemplated the severity of our situation. I wondered if God cared. I wanted to scream, "Hey God, do You know what's happening here? My baby is dying. Where are You?" I felt abandoned, but I said none of this out loud.

The friend from church that joined us that morning was a young woman that I barely knew. (She would become one of my dearest lifelong friends.) She, Gay, was studying Psalm 139 in Bible Study Fellowship, an incredible Bible study I'd eventually have the privilege to attend. She would've been at that Bible study, but because of that winter storm, the study was canceled. She felt led to come to the hospital and share that scripture with us. As I sat wondering if the Shepherd knew what was happening, she read out loud Psalm 139:13–16 from the Living Bible.

As I sat absorbed by overwhelming pain and hurt, I heard these words,

> You made all the delicate, inner parts of my body,
> and knit them together in my mother's womb.
> Thank you for making me so wonderfully complex! [It is amazing to think about.]
> Your workmanship is marvelous—how well I know it.
> You watched me as I was being formed in utter seclusion,
> as I was woven together in the dark of the womb.
> You saw me before I was born.
> Every day of my life was recorded in your book.
> [How precious it is, Lord, to realize that You are thinking about me constantly!]
>
> Psalm 139:13–16a (NLT)

And I knew that God had reached out to us in a mighty way. He knew exactly what was happening. He saw Jan's heart defect before she was born and numbered the days of her life. Light pierced through the darkness that held me captive as He sent His Word and began to heal my heart that cold winter morning. I was so in awe of His love at that moment that I fell to my knees and prayed out loud.

"Father, I forgot that twelve days ago, when Jan was born, we dedicated her to You in our prayer time. All week I've prayed either heal my child or take my child. I'd forgotten that I'd already given her to You and that she's Yours to start with, not mine. You love her far more than I do. I place her back in Your arms and ask that Your will be done."

Mike prayed a very similar prayer, and the atmosphere of that room was suddenly electric with God's presence. It was as if we'd all been transported into a tent of His glory as that little chapel was permeated with His peace. I felt I could almost reach out and touch the hem of His garment. Joy exploded in my heart as He lifted the heavy burden I'd attempted to carry on my own. It was miraculous to have that weight removed!

As peace and joy burst through the darkness, I truly was astounded. I said out loud, "I don't know what just happened to me," and I described what I was feeling.

My pastor said, "Pam, that is the peace that passes all understanding."

Our circumstances hadn't changed. Our baby was still dying, but on my knees at the altar, I'd exchanged that spirit of heaviness for the beautiful garment of praise. And I learned that day as I prayed that where King Jesus is, there truly is peace…even when the storm still rages! Wow! And that peace truly does pass all understanding—no matter what you're going through.

And that scripture became my life scripture that I quote quite often. It applies to each of us. God had seen not only Jan in my womb when she was being formed, but he'd seen me in my mother's womb also. He knew what Jan and I would face, and He'd already graced each of us with the giftings we'd need to navigate our hard places. What an incredible verse to store in my toolbox of hope.

Another miracle took place that morning, too, as we prayed. Mike's sister and mom sat quietly on the back pew as the rest of us knelt down front. Terri, his sister, had been searching for answers for a long time. She knew something was missing from her life because she felt an emptiness inside. When the sweet presence of the Shepherd saturated the chapel, she met her Savior for the first time. All because of a helpless, little seven-pound baby lying upstairs in a coma, another sheep was born into the kingdom.

Already we could see that God was using this dire situation to bring forth His glory. From the experience of the chapel, Mike's mom was also touched and would later pen the beautiful poem that follows:

"For Janice Marie"

You sent us a little one
From your home up above
And in no time at all
She captured our love.
So tiny, so precious
And ever so dear
It seemed like a miracle
That we had her here.

Did we take her for granted,
As we all tend to do?
Did we seem to forget,
This gift was from you?
Was our faith so complacent,
Did we fail to give praise?
Did we need a reminder,
You could number her days?
Dear God, in your wisdom
You brought us down low
Made us all realize
We needed you so
As each day grew darker
We pleaded with You

And hard though it was
Knew what we must do.
Our hearts seemed to know
She belonged to you.
When we accepted Your will
Your Peace came through.
Now each day grows brighter
And we know, You are near.

We know you are with us
We have nothing to fear.
So, thank You, dear God
For showing the way.
May we never forget
Now we've learned how to pray.

Jean Marie Goddard

Renewed and at peace, we faced the doctors, prepared for whatever they might say. They told us the test showed some brain activity, so thankfully, we were never asked to sign the papers to take Jan off life support. Once again, all we could do was wait and trust. Little did we know God had yet another miracle to perform that day.

The Salesman

Mike hadn't been in his office all week. Later that day, an overly ambitious salesman decided that he would come to the hospital in an effort to get business. He arrived just as it was time to visit the ICU. Without thinking, Mike invited him to go back to the unit with him.

I was standing beside Jan when I saw Mike bring in this tall, tanned stranger. The man was earnestly giving his sales pitch as he walked up to Jan's incubator. He abruptly stopped in mid-sentence when he saw Jan, and the color drained from his face. I told Mike later that we'd better prepare anyone else who thought they wanted to see Jan. The man left shortly without mentioning business again. Little did we know that God was using Jan to reach a man whose heart had long since been hardened toward Him.

The day ended with Jan still dying, but His presence and peace remained firmly planted in our hearts. That evening the tanned salesman's wife called.

"Mrs. Whitley, you don't know me, but I felt that you should know what has happened at our home today. I've prayed for my husband for years. Not only did he not share my faith, but he also refused to have anything to do with God or church. Actually, he's led a pretty rough life. Today he came home early. He asked me to please teach him to pray because a little girl at Children's hospital desperately needed his prayers."

She said together they'd gotten down on their knees and prayed for Jan. I cried and praised God again that He was using such a painful situation for His glory. And for months and months afterwards, this man would visit Jan at our home. He was sure his prayers had saved her life—and who knows, they may have!

Prepared for a Funeral

Friday, Jan's heart rate began to slow down, and her kidneys ceased to function. The doctors told us she was dying. I called my two brothers in Mississippi and my sister in Alabama. They left immediately for Oklahoma, prepared for the funeral of the little niece they'd never met. That night Mike and I went home to spend time with Ben and wait for my family's arrival. I slept very little, expecting a call at any moment from the hospital.

Saturday morning, I woke up early, comforted by the fact that my brothers and sister had arrived. For some reason, a melody ran through my mind, complete with words, "It took a miracle of love and grace." My husband woke with a tune playing in his mind also, "Do you believe in miracles? So do I." We both thought it was strange, but neither of us mentioned it to the other until later that day.

We quickly dressed and made our way once again to Children's. To our astonishment, Jan had started to wake up. Her heart rate was now normal, and her kidneys had begun to function again. Before the day was over, the doctors called it a miracle. By evening, Jan was totally awake and sucking on her respirator. We knew God had given her back. We didn't know what the future held, but we certainly knew Who held the future, and we knew we'd trust Him no matter what lay ahead!

In less than twenty-four hours after coming out of the coma, Jan was breathing on her own and drinking ten ccs of formula every hour. She progressed rapidly. However, there were very obvious signs of brain damage. She still had seizures, and her eyes occasionally rolled back in her head as her body shuddered. She was placed on phenobarbital. Her left arm was drawn backwards and turned awkwardly towards her back, and more symptoms soon became apparent. At this point, we were so elated to have our baby back that we barely noticed.

Within a few days, we were able to take Jan home a second time. She'd been in the hospital for almost a month. As we left Children's Hospital, we discussed the probability of Jan's brain damage. We thought with hard work, we'd help Jan overcome most of the challenges that lay in her future. We were very, very naive.

We didn't have a clue as to what was ahead or that our real battle had just begun. We didn't realize that our lives would be forever changed. We just knew God had given our baby back. Armed with a heart full of faith and love, minus any medical training, we began the twenty-four-hour a day care of our critically brain-injured child. Another new journey had begun.

God's Grace Keeping Pace

God's grace was shed on us richly during this time in our lives. We were amazed as we saw people saved because of Jan, and one of the most lifelong graces gifted to us was Psalm 139. It would be our anchor through many trials as we applied it to Jan's life and to our own.

> You watched me as I was being formed in utter seclusion,
>   as I was woven together in the dark of the womb.
>   You saw me before I was born.
> Every day of my life was recorded in your book.
>   Every moment was laid out
>   before a single day had passed.

[It's His grace for you too! Let's keep looking for glimpses of His grace.]

Psalm 139:15–17 (NLT)

Chapter 6
JESUS, TAKE THE WHEEL

"Thus says the Lord to you, 'Do not be afraid and do not be dismayed at this great horde, for the battle is not yours but God's'" (2 Chronicles 20:15b, ESV).

Coming home from the hospital wasn't quite the celebration we'd envisioned. Jan was still an extremely sick little girl. She'd contracted a staph infection in her incisions a few days before we left the hospital. (In addition to the heart surgery incision, they'd made a small slit in the groin area for the catheterization.) The doctors had taken out the stitches so the wounds could be cleaned deeply twice a day with peroxide. They told us we could go home a few days early if we'd learn that procedure.

Mike took the initiative and said he'd be responsible for that part of her care. The nurse showed him what to do, using a Q-tip soaked in peroxide and cleaning inside the open wound until it bled. When I saw my tenderhearted husband almost faint as the color drained from his face, I knew I'd need to do that. It was one of many new things we'd face and need to learn how to handle.

Jan would scream for hours after the Q-tip procedure. Anything that agitated her (and that certainly did) would have that effect. I'd try everything I could think of to calm her down, but nothing seemed to work. She was like a child with the colic; only it lasted fifteen to eighteen hours every day! If she was allowed to cry for long, she'd become progressively more and more hysterical—until she was sick. Not only would she throw up, but her damaged thermostat would cause her temperature to steadily climb. I had to find some way to calm her.

Each day became an exercise in problem-solving. Feeding Jan was one of the hardest things to do. She had a very weak sucking reflex and a lot of congestion. In between the screaming, she'd struggle and struggle to take her bottle. She'd swallow so much air that she'd throw up most of what I fed her. Finally, someone who heard of our plight sent several three-ounce syringes via a friend. I learned to feed Jan with them, drop by drop. They were lifesavers.

Another major problem came with Jan's medications. Dosages of Dilantin and phenobarbital were given at nine in the morning and nine at night for the seizures. She always choked and threw up part of the dosage. I was never certain how much of the medication she'd thrown up or how much I needed to re-give.

It was a fight for survival—for both Jan and me. The days stretched into seemingly endless nights and the endless nights into endless weeks. If anything, Jan's health deteriorated, and my physical strength was taxed to the limit. It slowly sank in that I was facing the fiercest battle of my life, and the battle had only just begun.

Fortunately, I'd learned to trust the Shepherd enough during my dad's sickness that I didn't have a reoccurrence of colitis. I determined in my heart that this tragedy would not destroy our family. God would be our strength, and He'd carry us through this storm.

It was up to me, however, to commit my burden to Him. Normally I'd have spent extra time reading my Bible, but this storm was so intense that the opportunity to read wasn't there because almost every moment was spent trying to keep Jan calm. I had to develop other avenues to hear His voice. He showed me very quickly what those avenues were. I bought Christian tapes and albums and listened to Christian radio. By those means, I kept His Word flowing almost twenty-four hours a day, and my heart and mind fixed on Him. Time and time again, the Shepherd would speak to me and strengthen me when I thought I couldn't go on.

One night as it neared the time to give Jan her phenobarbital, I found myself tense and teary. The phenobarbital had such a strong alcohol content that it always choked Jan, no matter how carefully I gave it to her. Usually, she'd become hysterical as I tried to give it to her and eventually throw up most of the medicine.

As I prepared her medication, dreading even the thought of attempting to give it to her, I heard the words of one of my new records playing in the background. It was as if the words separated themselves from the music, and I heard them loud and clear.

When you go out to fight, the Lord is going to fight for you because the battle is not yours! It was as if the Lord said to me, "Pam, you are trying once again to fight this battle in your own strength—to carry this burden alone. Give it to Me."

"Lord, I will gladly give it to You, but I don't know how You are going to solve this one."

The next day, I went to the pharmacy to have Jan's prescription refilled. The pharmacist asked why I was giving her the liquid phenobarbital.

"Do you mean there is another form?"

To my great joy, he showed me a small white flavorless pill that could be easily crushed, and our medication problem was over. *Thank You, Lord.*

Little by little, it began to sink in that the little girl that was born on January 1 was gone forever. My brain-damaged child barely resembled our New Year's baby, but I loved her even more. I'd never witnessed anyone struggle so much to live, and it brought forth the fight in me. Whatever it took, whatever God's plan was, with Him, I was prepared for war. And war it was!

Night after night, Jan continued to cry. Sleep for her was only in bits and pieces and normally only while I stood under the spotlight over our fireplace, cradling her in my arms, swaying her from side to side. For some strange reason, that calmed her. I swayed her to feed her and swayed her to calm her. Swaying became my new way of life. It was also a great way to lose weight. I should have patented it and sold it as a new weight loss program.

I realized so many things I'd previously taken for granted. Sleep became a thing I did occasionally when my body would push no further. Stress became a way of life and exhaustion my permanent partner. In the midst of everything, I still attempted to be a good wife. I was a Southern gal, and I had high expectations of myself. I still cooked full-course meals and set the table each evening. I still kept the house in order, and I attempted to do the normal things with Ben that I'd always done. But I literally felt so detached from my life that it was as if I was standing back watching myself living those endless days and nights. They slowly slipped by, and I wasn't sure Jan or I'd survive!

We had an appointment scheduled for Jan in February to go to a local clinic whose specialty was brain-damaged children. I hung my hope on that appointment. I thought if I could survive until then, they'd know what to do. They were experts with answers. I hadn't learned that God was our sole source of provision and help.

The appointed day finally arrived. After four long hours of questions and tests from six or seven specialists, we were informed that Jan had brain damage. We sat there rather stunned—of course, Jan has brain damage—we'd told them how and when it occurred. Four hours later and four hundred dollars poorer, their diagnosis was, "Your daughter has brain damage!"

Before that could sink in, another person said, "Please step into our business office, and we will assign a counselor to your case."

We mechanically did what they requested. Seated in yet another office, our assigned counselor began to ask rather personal questions about our marriage. Mike and I looked at each other, wondering what in the world we'd gotten ourselves into.

When we seemed rather offended at the array of personal questions, the counselor said rather adamantly, "Parents with brain-damaged children need counseling. We will help you accept that your child is brain-damaged." I wanted to say, "I'm not having trouble accepting Jan's brain damage—I'm having trouble keeping her and myself alive!" I kept quiet.

"Besides that," she continued with an air of superiority, "a high percentage of marriages end in divorce when a handicapped child is involved!"

Great, just the kind of encouragement we need right now. We sat blankly staring at our "counselor" as she mapped out their new plan for our lives.

They expected us to drive to their clinic (which was a forty-five-minute drive) twice a week so they could work with Jan and counsel us. Mike and I just looked at each other again. We realized they had no inkling of the struggle we were facing—just to live. To them, we were just another case. We'd tried to tell them what we were going through, but it was as if their ears were deaf. I was so exhausted; it wouldn't have been safe for me to drive across town weekly to see them. As for our marriage, Jan's battle had brought us closer together than ever.

What we needed wasn't what they were offering. What a terrible disappointment! We left and, for the first time, faced that there probably was no help nor anyone who understood our battle. How I longed to talk to even one parent who had walked in our shoes, someone who had survived and understood our struggle. One day, I'll write a book for other parents to read—one day—if I survive!

That night at about 2:00 a.m., as I stood under the spotlight swaying Jan—side to side under the fireplace spotlight—anger welled up inside me. I sobbed, *God, why did this have to happen to our child? Why? Oh, Lord, why? Why? Why did this have to happen to our lives?* Suddenly, something miraculous and amazing happened. God showed me His only Son, Precious Jesus, hanging on that old rugged cross. I saw the blood dripping from His head, His hands, and His feet. And God spoke to my heart, *Is the servant greater than the One he serves?*

I grasped with what Jesus had done for me…at least as much as my finite mind could. He, Jesus, had chosen to exchange His home in glory for an earthly body—knowing that He'd suffer and die on that old rugged cross. He'd chosen it because of His love for His creation. He willingly became our sacrifice. I cried tears of repentance as

I asked God to forgive me. Why on earth would I expect my life to be without pain when even the Son of God's life wasn't? I would never again ask, "Why me? Why not me!"

I determined that Jan's life would not be wasted. My cry changed to use me as I began to learn that He was truly my only source of help. He who had suffered, bled, and died for me was the only one who could understand my struggle and be my strength. He was the only One who could truly help us.

Hope Lost

Medically, the next problem we faced was to get Jan's seizures under control. They were constant—breaking through night and day. We were sent to a well-known neurologist who had written several books. On my scheduled appointment day, I went alone since Mike had taken off work so many times in the past three months. Little did I know that this would be another very upsetting appointment. It wasn't that I expected to be encouraged, but I'd hoped to get help with the terrible seizure activity and direction in handling our crisis.

This expert ran his tests, all the while treating Jan like a sack of potatoes. This upset me. Brain-damaged or not, Jan was a precious little girl and my daughter, who I loved dearly. She wasn't some defective toy.

When the tests were complete, he sat down and delivered some of the most discouraging news any parent can hear.

"Your child will never smile or respond in any way. She is severely brain-damaged. You need to place her in a facility and get on with your lives."

That wasn't what I was expecting to hear. I was stunned, to say the least, and could only come back with what I knew as fact. "Doctor, Jan does respond. I've seen her smile several times. It's normally early in the morning when she first wakes up."

Looking rather cynically at me and talking to me like I was a child, he said, "Mrs. Whitley, many parents see things they want to see." He looked back at Jan, again treating her as if she was damaged merchandise. I wanted to scream at him, "She's our little girl, not some broken object you discard." Instead, I asked about seizure medication and anything else that might help her.

Relieved when I was able to leave his office, I rushed home to the privacy of my bedroom to be alone with God. Throwing my weary body across the bed, I cried and cried, pouring out my tears and my heart to God. Will this heartache ever end? This seemed more than I could endure.

After that negative word, I became disheartened. Once again, I listened to the voice of fear, turning my eyes to my circumstances rather than God and His Word. I would learn that a victory won once was not necessarily a victory that I'd triumph in continually. I'd have to learn time and time again how to climb back out of that pit of self-pity. Once again, I began to go through the motions of living, and without realizing it, I accepted that our situation was hopeless. I lost my faith and hope.

But God always meets His children right where they are. How I praise Him that He is so faithful; He will never leave us without help, He will never give up on us, He always knows where we are, and He knows what we need.

One morning I picked up a devotional book and began to read. God spoke as I read these words: *resignation to My will is a greater barrier than unbelief.* I read it a number of times before the truth of it finally sank in. Resignation to *My will is a greater barrier than unbelief.*

I saw it. I'd resigned myself to the fact that my life would never be any different—that Jan's life would never be any different. I'd believed every negative word the doctor said, and in doing so, I'd lost my hope—when there is no hope, there is no faith. Have you ever been there?

I had stopped trusting God to work in our situation…the very thing I'd said I wouldn't do. I'd stopped expecting Him to take something hopeless and work it to our good. I, in fact, had closed the door to His blessings by my despondent attitude and resignation. I was walking in self-pity rather than in faith, and I hadn't recognized it.

I once again remembered that God had given Jan back and that He had a plan that I could trust.

God forgive me for my lack of faith. I don't believe that You gave Jan back to never smile or enjoy life. Please let her know the joy of being loved and let her experience happiness. Let her smile and laugh and enjoy her life.

Since I was certain God had given her life back, I wouldn't believe that He wanted her to be like a vegetable, never responding or smiling. I wouldn't believe the negative report I'd received from the neurologist either. I'd believe God!

For several mornings, I waited by the crib with my camera. Sure enough, one morning when Jan first awoke, I captured several very sweet smiles on film. No one could ever convince me again that Jan wouldn't ever smile or respond, nor could they tell me I was only seeing things. I had tangible proof!

As my attitude changed, my joy returned, and I stepped back into the battle. You see, resignation takes you out of the battle. The scriptures say in Matthew 18:18a (NIV), "Things that are bound on earth are bound in heaven" (paraphrased). I'd bound things up by not believing for anything. I'd forgotten that Jesus said that He came to give abundant life and that with Him, nothing is impossible. I'd forgotten that He said that what I committed to Him, He'd work to my good. One step at a time, He was teaching me to keep my eyes on Him and believe His Word, no matter what.

I learned that looking into the face of Jesus lifted me above my circumstances. I played one song over and over in my heart—*"Turn your eyes upon Jesus / look full into His wonderful face / and the things on earth will grow strangely dim in the light of His glory and grace."*

I also wrote a definition for resignation so that I could read it often in case resignation attempted to grab hold of me again: Resignation puts God in a box by saying, "My situation is hopeless." Resignation says, "I accept this, but I can't see how anything good could come out of it." Resignation is disappointment with "my lot in life." Ultimately, resignation focuses on painful circumstances and feeling sorry for self. True acceptance trusts God, in spite of what I see. True acceptance knows God can work even this to my good and expects God to move. True acceptance focuses on God (not circumstances) and continues to praise Him with an expectant heart! And I've come to believe another word for true acceptance is hope in Christ.

God's Grace Keeping Pace

God is with us in our hard places even when it doesn't feel like it. I learned He'd provide in ways I couldn't imagine; I just had to keep looking for those glimpses of His grace and never give in to self-pity. Self-pity is a joy robber, peace stealer, and hope killer.

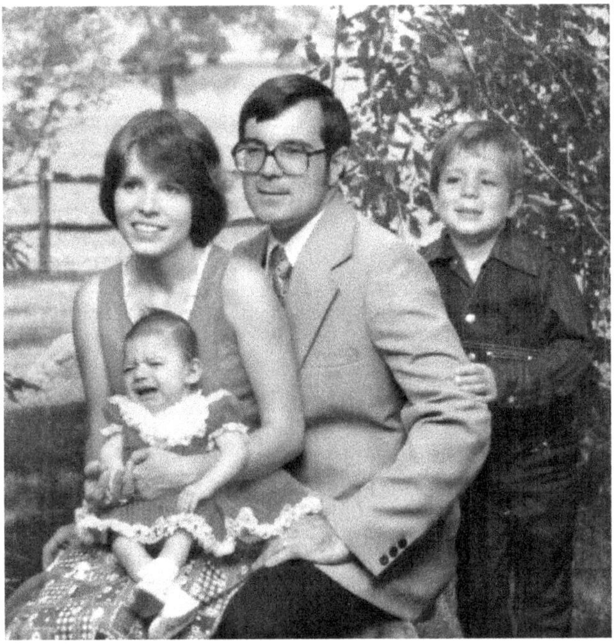

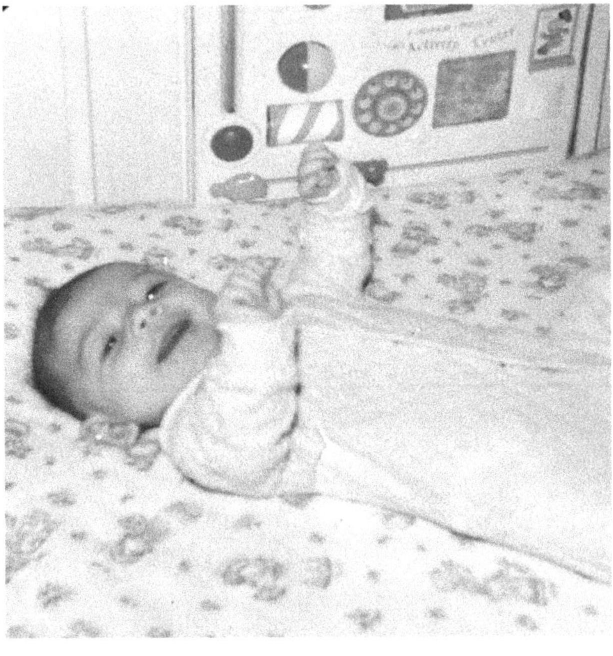

Chapter 7
MY WEAPON

"The weapons of our warfare are not physical [weapons of flesh and blood]. Our weapons are divinely powerful for the destruction of fortresses" (2 Corinthians 10:4, AMP).

My mom stayed until spring that year after Jan's birth, and she was a godsend. She read to Ben when my days were overflowing with responsibilities. She helped with the laundry and cleaning if needed and took a turn walking Jan while I cooked dinner. She did so much.

But as spring approached, she had many responsibilities on the farm that she had to attend to. Without her, at that time, I had no one who could keep Jan. I still needed, on occasion, to attend business functions with Mike, and Ben had school activities as well that I wanted to be a part of. Taking Jan along was usually out of the question because she still cried so much.

Lord, please send someone to help me.

A few Sundays later, when I took Jan to our church nursery, a new volunteer welcomed us. She seemed really at ease with Jan—which was unusual. She was able to keep her calm too. I visited with her afterwards, and she shared a bit about herself, "I've just retired, but I have always worked and kept myself busy. I could use some extra income, and I dearly love children. If you know of anyone who needs a babysitter, or if you need one, here's my telephone number." Wow.

Before I knew it, I had a new friend and grandmother to fill in for my mom. Mother would leave on April 8, so Nell came for the first time on April 6 to get better acquainted with Jan and meet Ben. God was teaching me, step by step, that He would provide when I prayed.

A new excitement was in my heart. I could see that God was at work. *Lord, I don't know what your plan for Jan is, but show me what I need to do. I don't want to waste my suffering or hers. Please guide us.*

A few days later, an article in the newspaper grabbed my attention. It was about a brain-damaged boy who lived in Oklahoma City. He was on an intensive program taught to his parents by a clinic in Philadelphia, Pennsylvania. Many volunteers came into their home daily to help implement the program, and the parents shared about the improvement they'd seen. I knew that I must talk with them.

Laying the article aside, I planned to call the parents later. Jan was four months old, and Ben was now five. Each day was full of so much chaotic activity that I lost the article, and I couldn't remember the names of the parents. I was crushed.

Lord, I need to talk to those parents. Please help me find them.

The last week in April, the house down the street sold. I walked over to greet the new people after they'd settled in. During our visit, I told them about Jan, and they told me about a man from work who had a little boy who was brain-damaged. In fact, they said, "There was an article in the paper a few weeks ago that talked about the special program they do!" They gave me the couple's number. *Thank you, Lord!*

We met Ron and Donna Cooper in just a few days. They were wonderful. Finally, someone not only knew what we were going through but had faced the same brick wall we'd faced and had found help for their child. They encouraged us and taught us what they had already learned. We felt God was guiding us in the direction of The Institute in Philadelphia. We continued to pray, asking God if this was for us.

Only two days later, I stopped at my favorite Christian book store to pick up a devotional book that I frequently bought to give as gifts. A friend waited in the car with the kids as I raced in to grab the book. I knew exactly where it was located and rushed directly to it. Beside it, with the cover facing outward, stood a hardback book with the picture of a beautiful little girl on the front. Her dark hair and olive complexion reminded me of Jan.

I read the title—*Tara: The Dramatic Story of a Brain-Injured Child's Courageous Fight to Get Well*. I gasped, and my heart pounded. Only days before, I'd called that small book store, asking if they had any books specifically about a brain-damaged child. They had searched and found nothing. I knew this book was for me.

I probably broke the speed limit that day racing home so I could read this little girl's story. As I read the story of the parents who were about our age, and were married the same length of time as us, and had two healthy children—a boy and a girl, I cried. I read the horror of an accident that left Tara brain-damaged. I turned the page as I hurt for them and identified with them with every sentence. I gasped as I read of their being led by God onto a program in Philadelphia called The Institutes. Wow! This had to be where God was leading us.

I called The Institute for the Achievement of Human Potential the next day. They were very helpful, but they were a highly sought-after program. In fact, people came from all over the world with their broken and hopeless children. The first available appointment was two years away, but they put us on a waiting list. They explained that many kids died because they didn't live to make their appointment, so the list would change. Would Jan be one of the names removed from the list because she didn't live to get there?

We needed help now. Our church and others began to pray that we'd get to the Institute sooner than the appointed day. As I completed reading about Tara, I also realized that if we were able to get on the program, I would be embarking on the most difficult thing I'd ever attempted. In fact, it was called by the parents and the Institute the hardest program in the world.

Every part of me cried out, "I don't want to do this. It's too hard," but at the same time, my inner spirit cried out, "You must do this." I knew in my heart that I must do it not only for the sake of Jan but for the sake of our whole family. Even though I knew the program would consume almost every waking hour, Jan's care already did that anyway. If this could eventually give our family a chance for even a semblance of a normal life, I felt I must do it. More important than that, it seemed to be a part of God's plan.

While we prayed for our appointment to be sooner, the Coopers helped us develop our own abbreviated program. In order to get volunteers, I had to ask for help. That was hard and uncomfortable.

Summer was just beginning, and with it, the long summer break. I found that teenagers were delighted to help "pattern" Jan, so my first volunteers were both boys and girls who lived in our neighborhood. Soon, they brought their parents. Finally, we were doing something to help Jan! (Patterning...simulates crawling by moving a person's limbs for them...done on a special counter height padded table...requiring three to five people.)

We knew that once we had our first appointment in Philadelphia, all of our vacation time would be spent for return trips to the Institute, so we decided that before starting the full-fledged program, we'd take a trip to Mississippi. Our pastor was in the National Guard. He had a two-week training session in Mississippi, only forty-five minutes from my mother's farm. We all decided to go at the same time, and his family would stay out on the farm with us. It was a wonderful break.

Our pastor's wife, Phyllis, and I spent many hours in the cool of the morning sitting out front under the shade of the tall pines. As she shared her heart and her favorite scriptures, they'd become mine too. I loved when she shared Psalm 125:1–2 (NIV): "Those who trust in the Lord are like Mount Zion, which cannot be shaken but endures forever. As the mountains surround Jerusalem, so the Lord surrounds his people both now and forevermore." What a mentor she was to my hurting twenty-eight-year-old self. God again was mortaring stones of His grace via His saint.

Another special scripture she shared was John 17:20–21a (NIV): "My prayer is not for them alone. I pray also for those who will believe in me through their message, that all of them may be one, Father, just as you are in me and I am in you." As we read Jesus' prayer to His Father, I was so touched that He'd had me (and you) on His heart and prayed for me (us) before His crucifixion!

I wanted a study Bible like hers because mine didn't have the wonderful study help that hers did. She said her Pilgrim Edition was out of print, but we drove to a small shop in Columbia, and I was so excited that they still had one in stock, just like hers. It became my most cherished sidekick. The print is too small for me to see easily today, but I still refer to that Bible with a magnifying glass and love it.

That time of growing in God's Word would prepare me for yet another trial. We returned home on July 8. On July 10, Mike noticed blood in his urine. He immediately went to a kidney specialist. The doctor took several X-rays and came in with a very concerned look on his face.

"Mike, there appears to be a tumor on your kidney. We'll have to run tests to find out what this tumor is. We'll check you into the hospital as an outpatient as soon as we can."

That night Mike was very restless. We'd prayed together, but after I went to sleep, Mike continued to pray. He shared with me the next day that he'd knelt by the bed and prayed, "Father, for the sake of my family and what we're already going through, please heal me."

As he knelt, he felt an unmistakable change take place. Heat came over him and manifested itself in his lower back, where the tumor had showed up. It moved down to his knee, where he had an old injury. Afterwards, Mike was filled with a supernatural peace. The next morning, he eagerly told me that God had healed him. We went through with the tests anyway, but I told the doctor he'd find no tumor. I think he thought I was crazy. He kept Mike in the surgery room for quite a while. He couldn't find any sign of a tumor and was baffled because the X-rays had showed it clearly. It was gone. Praise God!

A Way We Knew Not

Meanwhile, Jan's health worsened. She was sick quite frequently, spiking high temps often, and the difficulty of keeping her food down seemed to grow worse. She still slept very little and suffered many seizures throughout the night. She was so frail that her legs looked like toothpicks. I'd be up with her as many as twenty to thirty times each night; that is, those nights that I actually went to bed. (My mom counted one night—or I'd have no idea.) I moved her into our bedroom so that I'd spare myself a few extra steps. It was a good thing both Mike and Ben were heavy sleepers, or no one would have gotten sleep in our household. As this continued, I knew I had to have definite direction from God. I was desperate to hear from Him.

One Sunday, I fasted and prayed and sought God in His Word with my whole being. I spent every spare moment all day reading the Bible and praying. I wanted God to know I was sincerely seeking Him for answers and help. About 10:00 p.m., I climbed into bed, propped a pillow behind my back, and prepared to read again. This time my Bible fell open to Isaiah 42:5–10, 16 (KJV). Something strange happened. It was as if the scripture came off the page, and someone read it to me:

> Thus saith God the Lord, he that created the heavens, and stretched them out; [And in my heart, I heard He who created Jan] he that spread forth the earth, and that which cometh out of it; He that giveth breath unto the people upon it, and spirit to them that walk therein:
>
> I the Lord, have called thee in righteousness, and will hold thine hand, and will keep thee, and give thee for a covenant of the people, for a light of the Gentiles;
>
> To open the blind eyes, to bring out the prisoners from the prison, and them that sit in darkness out of the prison house.
>
> I am the Lord: that is my name: and my glory will I not give to another, neither my praise to graven images.
>
> Behold, the former things are come to pass, and new things do I declare: before they spring forth, I tell you of them.

Sing unto the Lord a new song and His praise from the end of the earth.

And I will bring the blind by a way that they knew not; I will lead them in paths that they have not known; I will make darkness light before them, and crooked things straight. These things will I do unto them, and not forsake them.

Isaiah 42:5–10, 16 (KJV)

I knew God had spoken to me. I wasn't certain what He meant, but at that point, I felt He was going to heal Jan. His presence was so strong that my heart was totally flooded with His love. I'd said in times past that Jan's spirit was normal, but she was imprisoned by a body that didn't work because of a brain that was severely damaged. She was considered legally blind, and to my heart, these scriptures spoke of all those things and said, "He'd lead me in a way that I knew not."

A few weeks went by, and a sweet Christian neighbor that I respected invited us to attend a healing service with her. Since I was raised in a main-line denomination, I'd never gone to a healing service, and neither had Mike. I knew that there were many scriptures on healing and the Bible also says to some He gave the gift of healing. Could this be "the way we knew not"? Mike and I prayed about it and felt led to go. Our faith was in God and His Word as we trusted Him to guide us.

Our neighbor picked us up on the night of the service. The church was across town, and it took us a while to drive there. The young evangelist was already speaking when we arrived. We found seats in the balcony in the large, filled auditorium. As the service progressed, the preacher said, "I'd not planned to pray just for children tonight.

However, God has laid it on my heart that there are some very sick children here. If your child is ill, please come forward for prayer."

Mike quickly stood up and headed down front, as did quite a few other parents carrying their sick children. For some reason, I sat glued to my seat. The evangelist prayed individually for each child. The child next to Mike and Jan evidently had serious problems too. As the pastor prayed for the child, the mother began to weep. The minister asked her what was taking place. She described the presence of the Holy Spirit as a cool breeze surrounding her child. Her child appeared to have been healed.

The evangelist moved to Mike and Jan next. He immediately asked, "Where's this little girl's mother?" I raised my hand. "Sister, come down here."

Timidly, I rushed down to be with Mike and Jan.

Several people on whom he laid hands had fallen back as he prayed for them, so Mike braced himself, not knowing what to expect. The pastor placed his hand on Jan's heart, where all her problems had started (we'd not told him anything about her), and began to pray. Mike felt the power of God so mightily that He stumbled backwards, but he was determined not to fall.

The words that the evangelist spoke burned into my heart, "For these parents, I pray wisdom." That was all he said. *"For these parents, I pray wisdom!" I left thinking, Wisdom, wisdom, what wisdom? Lord, wisdom to go to the right doctor or the right church? Wisdom to pray the right prayer? What wisdom, God?*

Over a period of years, the Holy Spirit would teach me that the wisdom was Jesus and His precious Word, and His Word was my weapon to fight every storm that came our way. And He'd lead us with that precious Word "in a path we knew not."

God's Grace Keeping Pace

In our hard place, I learned that God heard my smallest cries, and He knew the weight of what I carried. Reading His Word continually equipped me to walk through my hard place and gave me strength and guidance. Let's keep looking for glimpses of His grace.

Chapter 8
PRAISE YOU IN THE STORM

"Trust in the Lord with all your heart, and do not lean on your own understanding. In all your ways acknowledge him, and he will make straight your paths" (Proverbs 3:5–6, NIV).

As the weeks flew by and the temps grew hotter, and the Oklahoma humidity rose; it was shocking to find that the weather had a terrible effect on Jan's seizures. One day I ran errands with both kids, and when we got back into the hot car, Jan began to seizure almost immediately. If we were outside for more than a few minutes when the temperature was over seventy, seizures would break through. Our world became the confines of our air-conditioned home. Someone had to stay with Jan if I needed to buy groceries if the temps were in the seventies. In spite of that, we patterned Jan twice a day and kept a fan blowing directly on her, and we kept the thermostat set low in the house.

I wondered if we'd make it to the Institute. In the late fall, we received a call telling us that Jan's appointment had been moved to February 19. We were elated. Now, if we survived a few more months, we'd have help.

In the meantime, the neurologist continued to increase Jan's seizure medication in an effort to control her seizures. Instead of them getting better, they got worse, particularly at night. I became so exhausted that I failed to wake up as quickly as needed.

Jan's seizures were called focal seizures. When one hit her, her little body became unbelievably stiff, and her head jerked involuntarily and painfully to her left. Her lip quivered, and the corner of her mouth pulled downward to the left as well as her left arm pulled behind her body as her eyes rolled back into her head. With each seizure, she'd scream out with a blood-curdling cry of pain. They horrified me.

I learned I could bring her out of the seizure if I was able to get her into a sitting position and lean her over. However, her body was inflexible, and she was strong, even though she was a skinny little thing. It took every ounce of strength I could muster to sit her up and then bend her rigid little body forward. As this continued night after night, I reached a point where I slept through the seizures that occurred nearer morning because I was too exhausted to wake up. Sleeping on the floor next to her seemed the solution, but toward dawn, I still didn't always wake up immediately.

By the time I would awake, Jan's fever would be 104°–106°F. I'd find her sweating profusely, and many times, not only would she have thrown up, but she would have bitten her mouth and been covered in blood as well. It was horrible. I'd grab her, fight to bend her body upright, run to the kitchen, sit her in the sink, and drench her with the sprayer and my tears as I attempted to bring her temperature down.

By December, as Jan neared her first Christmas and her first birthday, she was on so much seizure medication that she didn't respond to anything. She never smiled or even acted like she knew she was alive. Shopping for Christmas presents was an ordeal of sadness and grief.

As I walked down the aisles shopping for Ben's gifts, tears ran down my cheeks, and my knees shook a bit because I found myself on the aisle of the little girl's dolls. I knew Jan would pay them no attention. My heart ached as I remembered the Christmas before when we were expectantly awaiting her birth. How excited we'd been and what dreams we'd had. It seemed as if that Christmas was years ago, and I felt like an old woman. *God, will we ever be normal again?*

We decided to drive to Alabama and spend Christmas with my sister and her family. I was so exhausted and so close to our situation that I didn't realize how frail and sick Jan really was. I'm sure it was a hard trip on her little body. Thankfully, my mom met us there and rode back to Oklahoma with us. She'd spend the rest of the winter as she had the year before. After our return trip to Oklahoma, Jan cried all night. Her fever climbed higher and higher.

On her first birthday, we had no celebration. Instead, Jan was admitted to the hospital. Knowing how desperately I needed rest, our doctor deliberately placed Jan on a ward where I wasn't allowed to stay. Each morning, as I went to visit her, it grieved my heart to realize she didn't seem to recognize my presence.

Oh, God, will she ever know how much she is loved? Please, God, remember my prayer, let her know us and feel joy and love. Please allow her to be happy.

The Long-Awaited Trip

The Institute appointment that had seemed so far away finally arrived. Thankfully Jan had, for the most part, recovered from her first birthday hospitalization. The night before we left for our long-awaited appointment, we asked our deacons and church staff to come to our home and pray for Jan and us.

We based our request on James chapter 5—call the elders of the church. That was new for us and our deacon body (the laying on of hands), but they graciously consented to honor our request. As they gathered around Jan in our den and prayed, it was an encouraging time. It served as a reminder that our hope and faith were in God and what He'd do through the program.

The next day, on February 18, we flew into the Philadelphia airport for the first time. At thirteen months old, Jan weighed thirteen pounds and still wore newborn-sized clothing. For this trip, I'd made her a little long red dress with white lacy trim. Her legs still looked like toothpicks, and the long dress covered her legs. I sadly overheard someone say, "Look at that poor little baby; she is so sick."

Nonetheless, Jan had survived to make her appointment. That's what we'd been praying to happen. We checked into a hotel in Fort Washington, Pennsylvania, excited and scared over the new lifestyle we hoped to soon embark on.

We arose early the next morning. Our appointment was at eight thirty. We wanted to make certain we allowed plenty of time to find the Institute. To our dismay, an unexpected snowstorm had dumped fourteen inches of snow while we slept. We had trouble finding our rental car in the massive parking lot of snow-buried vehicles.

This was long before key fabs and alarm buttons were invented, so we relied on our bare hands to locate our snow-buried white rental car, and when we finally found it, we proceeded to dig it out with our gloveless hands. Mike warmed up the car, and we began our treacherous journey to Jan's appointment. At one point, we were stuck behind a long line of snowbound cars. Finally, Mike was so determined to get to our appointment on time that he drove up on the median and traveled some distance. I held Jan tightly and closed my eyes and prayed.

Finally, we were able to get back on the street. A little obstacle like fourteen inches of snow and a bunch of snowbound cars was not going to prevent us from making our long-awaited appointment.

Finally, 8801 Stenton Avenue loomed before us. Never had a sign been so thrilling to see—The Institutes for the Achievement of Human Potential. We'd made it in an unfamiliar rental car through fourteen inches of snow. Thank You, Lord.

The Institutes was housed in a neighborhood of sprawling, walled estates built in the early 1920s. The Institute itself was founded in 1955 and was internationally known for its pioneering work in brain development. They'd bought an old estate with many acres of land to expand. As we carefully turned into the long lane—the snow-blanketed grounds were an amazing site to our eyes. The expansive acreage was filled with huge old trees—pines, tall oaks, birches, and dogwoods, all blanketed in that thick fresh fourteen inches of snow. Only God could have created such an amazing winter wonderland.

We were the first to arrive that snowy morning, followed shortly by a couple from Italy. Before the day was over, we'd met parents and their broken children from all over the United States and the world. They'd come from South Africa, Italy, Germany, Japan, and Spain. Immediately, we shared a strong bond—we'd all brought our broken children that the world considered hopeless.

The Institute only accepts children with brain damage, so on the first day, they test to see who is suitable for the program. We were fairly certain that Jan would be accepted because we knew she had brain damage. That first appointment lasted until 2:00 a.m., almost eighteen hours! I was amazed at the expertise and care of the staff. No detail seemed to escape them. By the time that late-night appointment was over, we'd learned more about Jan's condition than we'd learned in the previous thirteen months.

We learned that Jan was profoundly brain-damaged, and her neurological age was that of a two and two tenths month old. By dividing her neurological age by her chronological age of thirteen months, we found that Jan was 16 percent of normal. The rest of the week, the specialist at the Institute developed a program for Jan and trained us to put it into effect. We'd attempt to train Jan's undamaged brain cells to assume the duties of her damaged cells. It'd be a very strenuous program, one that we'd daily execute from our home. It would require about sixty people a week to help put it into action, people that we'd train. We were ready for anything that would help Jan and our family.

After a week of intense training, we were both exhausted and exhilarated. We'd been on a downhill path for thirteen months, but now we had a set of instructions from people who seemed to know the way off that downhill descent. We left with goals to be reached and a path to get there. Plus, we would attempt to reach our first goal by our next visit in three months. We couldn't imagine how we were going to accomplish all that was expected of us. Equipment had to be built, and additional patterners found, but we knew with God's help we'd do it…and we did.

God's Grace Keeping Pace

In my hard places, God taught me how close He walked with me. He continually reminded me He held the future and He was worthy of my trust. Let's keep looking for glimpses of God's grace.

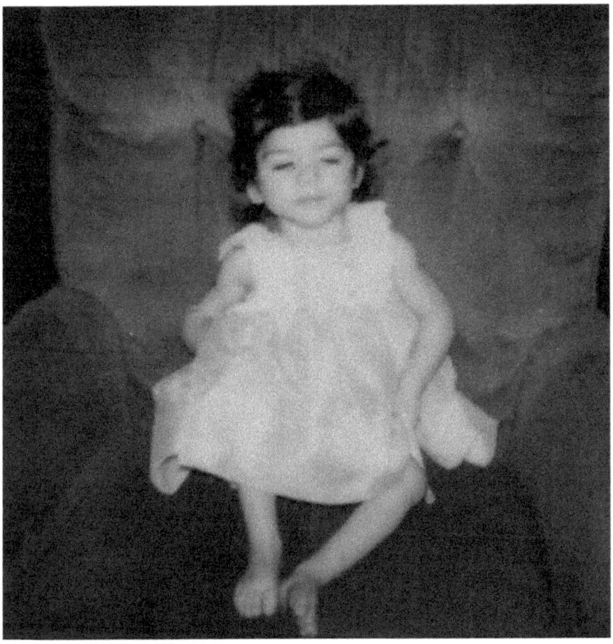

Chapter 9
KEEP WALKIN'

"Be strong and courageous. Do not be afraid or terrified because of them, for the Lord your God goes with you; he will never leave you nor forsake you" (Deuteronomy 31:6, NIV).

The Institute definitely equipped us with a huge goal—"to have Jan see, hear, and feel the world around her." In order to accomplish that, we had to grow Jan's visual, auditory, and tactile stimulation with increased *frequency, intensity,* and *duration*. The Institutes drilled those three words into us. We were starting with a thirteen-month-old whose sense of feel, sight, and taste was below the level of a newborn, so with frequency, intensity, and duration, we dove in with every fiber of our being! What a great creed that would be for Christians to follow—to spend time with God frequently, to intensely grab hold of His truths, and with duration to keep fighting the good fight of faith. Hmm, back to the Institute program.

The Institute's three objectives:

1. physical development ending in physical excellence;
2. intellectual development ending in intellectual excellence;
3. social development ending in social excellence.

They made no false promises, but every aspect of our new itinerary was to target one of those areas. Just as lifting weights develops biceps, hopefully, forcing the brain to receive messages would develop the brain. Every time we sent a message into the brain, hopefully, that pathway would grow. If that pathway grew, the brain would grow, and with it, Jan's head size would increase. There are five ways for the brain to take in information:

1) seeing,
2) smelling,
3) feeling
4) hearing, and
5) tasting.

A normal child learns by all these means. Watch a baby. He picks something up, and the first thing he does is put it into his mouth. He learns all about it quickly. He sees it, smells it, feels it, tastes it, and listens to it…all in a few seconds. It made sense that we'd have to do this for Jan.

She was locked inside a body that afforded her none of these opportunities. With our approach, we'd attempt to grow her brain by feeding it the information that she wasn't able to get on her own. In essence, that boiled down to us making Jan crawl, taste, smell, feel, and see. What a huge assignment!

By March, we had most of our patterners enlisted and our equipment built. We were ready for our new battle, but Jan wasn't. She fought us every step of the way. She was already a very irritable little girl. Now she was mad every second because we were forcing information into her brain, information she didn't want! She wanted to be left alone. We were as stubborn as she was and refused to let her stop us. It took extremely consistent tough love to input all this information into her little brain.

In a day, we were to pattern Jan (simulate crawling) fifteen times, five minutes each time. This sent the brain the message, "This is how it feels to crawl." Most children could be patterned with the help of only three people, but not Jan. Because of the resistance she put forth, patterning her demanded five sets of arms, two people on her right side and two people on her left side. Normally, I held Jan's head, turning it left and right as we crawled in place for her.

New people coming in couldn't believe that a thirteen-pound bony little thing like Jan could be so strong, but she was. Since each pattern was spaced fifteen minutes apart, we had three shifts set up for each day: 9:00 a.m., 1:00 p.m., and 3:30 p.m. Since I was the fifth patterner, that meant twelve women a day came through our home to pattern Jan.

Many of them were volunteers whom I met for the first time when they knocked at our door. These women gave an hour and a half of their precious time each week. Many of them continued for two years. What a touching sight to see, an assortment of women coming together for one reason. They'd heard that a helpless little girl and a family needed their assistance in order to see and feel her world. What wonderful women we met because of Jan. I still keep up with many of them today via FB today. Our family was forever blessed by their sacrifice of love.

And patterning (simulating crawling) was only a small part of Jan's day. Each day started at 6:00 a.m. for us—usually following a long night of seizures, restlessness, and little sleep for Jan or me. In addition to the patterns, Jan was to spend two hundred minutes a day face down on a visual stimulation device in a totally dark room. We achieved that darkness by lining the glass in the window with aluminum foil. The "light table," as we nicknamed it, was a box that was four feet long by three feet wide and fifteen and seven-eighths inches deep. The Institute gave us the design and the "how to build it" instructions. Seated inside the plywood box was a thousand watts of light, and the box was then covered with white plexiglass cut to fit the top. A friend helped us build it.

I sat right next to Jan, and I switched the light on for one second, then off for five to eight seconds, then on again—until it totaled a minute. (And this was using a regular light switch wired on the side of the box!) That had to be done a total of two hundred minutes a day. What a chore. Just keeping track of the seconds was an accomplishment, and writing it all down as the lights flashed was a challenge, but I did it. Jan was not crazy about being placed on top of that plexiglass on her tummy, looking down into those flashing lights either. But this told her brain this is how it feels to see. It wasn't only Jan's eyes that received a lot of training!

In addition, the Institute began a detoxification program, and we gradually reduced Jan's seizure medication each week. In its place, we substituted "masking." The mask was a small plastic sack with a plastic straw protruding from the end. We were told it was originally developed for astronauts by NASA. It was placed on Jan's face every seven minutes every waking hour for one minute, covering both her nose and mouth. This forced Jan to breathe deeply, thereby helping to develop her lungs. We were to mask her a total of eighty-four times per day and record each mask. A timer became a new attachment to my body along with my trusty record-keeping book.

And that wasn't our only visual stimulating exercise. Jan was to have a five-hundred-watt light flashed for a second in her eyes simultaneously with a pleasant taste. This was spaced out thirty times a day. A pleasant smell was introduced instead of a taste with the same light procedure thirty times a day. We collected all kinds of flavorings and perfumes that smelled like flowers, etc.

My patterners were wonderful and found additional items and brought them. With the same light, we introduced a pleasant touch ten times a day, too…cotton balls, fur, and any good feeling textured item met our requirements. Patterners helped with all those things—they were always on the lookout for things that would help us. What a beautiful thing to be a part of—all these women united in love to help a little girl. Forty years later, I still have those record books with those ladies' names recorded in them.

We also built Jan an inclined plane. This was a long wooden slide with a smooth surface that Jan had to "crawl" down. It was elevated just enough that any movement would cause Jan to scoot a little closer to the bottom. Hopefully, this would teach her the relationship between her arms, legs, and movement. As it became easier for her to go down the slide, we'd lower the height so that it took a little more work. Our starting height was sixteen inches.

Crawling, we learned, is a basic step in neurological development. Without proper crawling, there are areas of coordination that will never develop. The old saying "you must crawl before you can walk" held much more truth than I'd ever realized.

Another part of the program included "floor time." Jan was no longer allowed to lay on her back. She was to be on her tummy on the floor every second that we weren't working with her. I sewed a little garment for her. It looked like an apron from the front, and it closed with Velcro in the back and had Styrofoam rolls slid in sleeves on both sides extending to the back, and they wouldn't allow her to roll over… should she get to the point she could.

In addition to everything else, Jan was given a totally new diet. The Institute believed strongly that we must give Jan every advantage possible—in every area. Every morsel that entered her mouth needed to provide as much nutrition as we could pack in. Jan would never be introduced to any junk food. Twenty percent of her food was to be protein. Thirty percent was to be fat, and 50 percent was to be carbohydrates. I kept records of every morsel in order to insure she got everything she needed.

She was allowed no baby food, no salt, no sugar, and only twenty ounces of fluid a day. I didn't know then that Jan would never be able to tolerate solid foods. For the next thirteen years, I'd boil chicken every couple of days, puree it, and freeze it in ice cube trays. I'd do the same with fresh broccoli, squash, sweet potatoes, white potatoes, rice, and green beans. In addition to that, I fed her one yogurt a day (with active cultures) and plenty of bananas.

For breakfast, she had poached eggs and oatmeal. Every meal had protein and all the extra calories I could possibly pack in her diet. The Institute added many vitamins as well, including high doses of granulated vitamin C and B vitamins. It took me a while to locate the vitamins. Shaklee had the best quality liquid vitamins I could find, and a health food store carried a good granulated C. Those granulated and liquid vitamins were placed in each of Jan's feedings throughout the day. We'd indeed embarked upon a totally new lifestyle, and it felt good to be doing something for Jan's future and ours.

Needless to say, the program took about sixteen hours a day to accomplish. My breakfast became a quick protein shake loaded with vitamins to keep up my strength. Lunch, I learned to eat without ever taking time to sit down.

Any spare moment I had, I tried to give to Ben. My heart ached for my little boy, who had been the object of most of my time until the birth of Jan. He loved his little sister, but it had to be such a hard adjustment for him. All I could do was pray that God would protect his spirit and that he'd learn that we don't leave our wounded behind. If this tragedy had happened to him, he would've received the same measure of our love, attention, and affection. Kindergarten started for him the same year that we started to pattern. So much change, so fast for all of us!

My mom continued to spend about four to six months out of the year with us, and she helped keep the ice cube trays full of food and gave Ben much-needed extra love and attention. She answered the phone and helped me keep the household going. Without her self-sacrificing love poured generously into our lives, I don't think I could have continued at such a pace. She commented to me once that the great needs that Jan brought into our lives helped save hers because it gave her renewed purpose for living. She'd felt her life was over when my dad died. With the birth of Jan, she knew how much she was needed, and she emptied her life freely into ours.

When Mother wasn't with us, it was hard to stop to answer the phone when the program was in full swing. Mike bought us an answering machine. It was a rarity for even a business to have an answering machine in 1980, but when we were patterning, we couldn't stop to answer the phone. Many times, a patterner would call needing to find a substitute or ask a question. That machine helped me so much! Would you believe I still have it today, forty years later, in an upstairs closet? It has Mike's voice recorded on it and is one of my treasures of the past.

Back to the program, for all the efforts we put in, it seemed we were rewarded with fever and more fever. Since Jan fought so hard and because of her damaged "thermostat," we never knew if we were dealing with an infection or her damaged regulator. To say the program was hard is an understatement, but the stakes were high—we were fighting for Jan's life and the life of our family.

In my trusty keep-track-of-everything-record book, I find these notes:

> March 16, Jan woke up this morning with a 104°F temperature. Took her to doctor. March 17—Jan still running 104°F. March 18—still 104°F. March 19… Jan was very weak today but had no fever. She fought patterns. I allowed her to sleep and didn't wake her to mask—I will do only partial program until Jan regains strength. March 26…Jan running 104°F again…took to doctor. March 27—Jan awake almost all night. Fever 105°F…horrible night sweats even though she did not sweat off fever. Giving antibiotics three times a day…Jan is vomiting frequently. March 28. Fever 102°F. Three thirty—fever finally broke. March 31…We've been on the program for almost a month. In spite of all the sickness, I see an improvement in Jan's disposition. She definitely is not as cranky and irritable. She is still fighting patterning, but three of us are able to do it now. She is still weakened from her recent sickness and is croupy. April 3…Jan was awake all night last night. Began running 102°F in the night. Tried to pattern, but Jan fought so much that she threw up. April 4—patterned ten times today—Jan vomited several times. April 7—Jan woke up with a 102°F fever. Went back to sleep

after I gave her aspirin and slept two hours. Attempted three patterns, but Jan fought so much that we had to stop.

By this point, I really wondered if we could continue this program. We were seldom able to get everything done because of Jan's health. Yet, I felt this was where God had led us. "Lord, what do we do now?" I asked.

Once again, He answered me. I turned on the television while I was feeding Jan as an evangelist happened to give three alternatives to any struggle. His grace truly does keep pace. Here's what he said:

1) give up,

2) wait, and

3) fight.

We'd already waited thirteen months, and that got us nowhere. If I quit, that would leave us nowhere, so I knew we must continue to fight. As cruel as our daily, unrelenting routine seemed, I would keep pushing forward and choose daily the seemingly impossible path before us.

On April 11, we went back to the heart specialist for a check-up. As we sat in another small room, the doctor said, "Jan will probably not live to be three. She will die of pneumonia because of her underdeveloped lungs. If she does live, she can't live past age twelve because of the hole that is still in her heart."

Would we ever be able to crawl out of our valley? All I knew was that we must take one day at a time and continue to fight and place our future with God. Going back to my notes once more, I'm reminded of what we had to overcome on our hard path:

> April 15, Easter morning...Jan running 102°F...slept very little last night. April 16...Jan running a 105°F ...She had seizures about every ten minutes...sweated heavily... took her to doctor. He gave her a gamma globulin shot and will give her one monthly.
>
> April 17...bad night. Seizures...fever. April 25... bad night 103°F fever...April 26...fever...April 27-29 fever. Dr. Biehler gave Jan a shot. April 30...Jan had bad night...slept very little... Fever 104°F at 5:00 a.m. May 1...Jan is finally feeling better. She had a good night. Dr. Biehler has given her a shot three days in a row. Will continue through May 9. May 5...fever again. Gave aspirin and continued program. June 1. We're getting ready for our return visit to the Institute. We leave tomorrow. Jan has been sick most of this week—running a high fever, particularly at night. She seems to be over that now. She has started to frown and pucker up her bottom lip if her feelings get hurt...it's really cute. She has started to smile when her daddy whistles for her. She has cut two molars and is cutting a side tooth. She holds herself up well on both arms if I place them in front of her. June 2—flew to Philadelphia once again. I read a book on the flight up by a mother of a brain-damaged child. That mother's favorite scripture was Psalm 125:1-2. That's my special scripture from our summer visit in Mississippi a year ago... We had a layover in Kan-

sas City. Mike went to get us a coke. As he walked back up, Jan smiled in response to seeing her daddy! Thank You, thank You, Lord! Arrived.... except we got lost driving from the airport to our hotel. Once in the hotel...I could hardly believe it...the Gideon Bible was laying open to Psalm 125:1-2. What a comfort! God, You are so faithful. Again, thank You, Lord.

"Those who trust in the Lord are like Mount Zion, which cannot be shaken but endures forever. As the mountains surround Jerusalem, so the Lord surrounds His people both now and forevermore" (Psalm 125:1–2, NIV).

How wonderful it was to be back at the Institute. We were reunited with most of the thirty parents and children we started out with that snowy day in February. Some of the children had changed remarkably. Most had improved. It was exciting to see.

In spite of the fact that Jan had run a fever thirty-one of those days on the program, she had still improved 105 percent. Her weight had increased to sixteen pounds, but her greatest improvement was in her chest growth. She'd gone from wearing newborn clothing to size twelve months clothes in only three months. The masking was developing her lungs. Even her head had grown. With all of the fever and sickness, this was a remarkable change.

But what happened later was miraculous. Back in our motel room, free from our grinding schedule, we saw a Jan we'd never seen before. She was very playful and alert. We were thrilled when she turned over from her tummy to her back. We clapped and said, "Yea, Jan." And again, she smiled from ear to ear. This was such an incredible, incredible blessing that brought joy and tears. It was amazing to see her responding and happy…the same little girl the neurologist said would never smile or respond. It made all the torture she and we had endured worth it all. Jan, indeed, was beginning to see and feel her world. *Thank You, Lord. What if I'd believed the doctor's dreary outlook?* That frequency, intensity, and duration were working. We must keep on walkin'!

God's Grace Keeping Pace

God led us to the Institute, and there we found other parents fighting the same battle we were. They were such a blessing. We weren't meant to go through hard seasons alone. And among His most amazing graces occurred when Jan started to smile in response to her world and delight in sounds. I learned that when I pressed into the Lord and asked Him to renew my strength, He did. He'll do the same for you. Let's keep looking for glimpses of His grace.

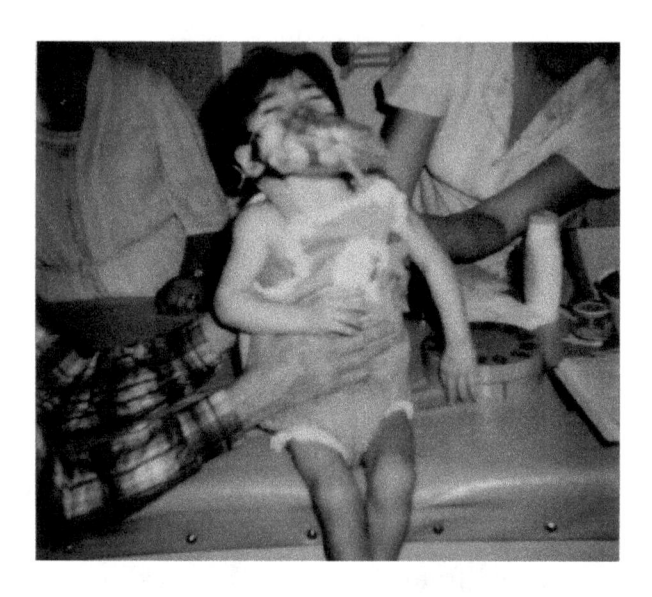

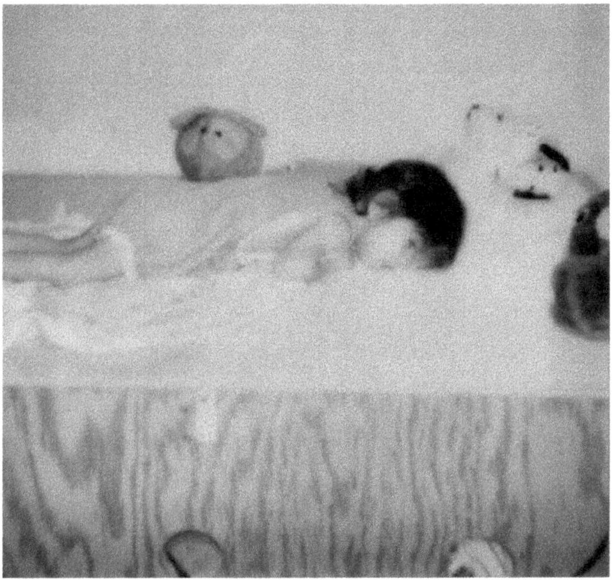

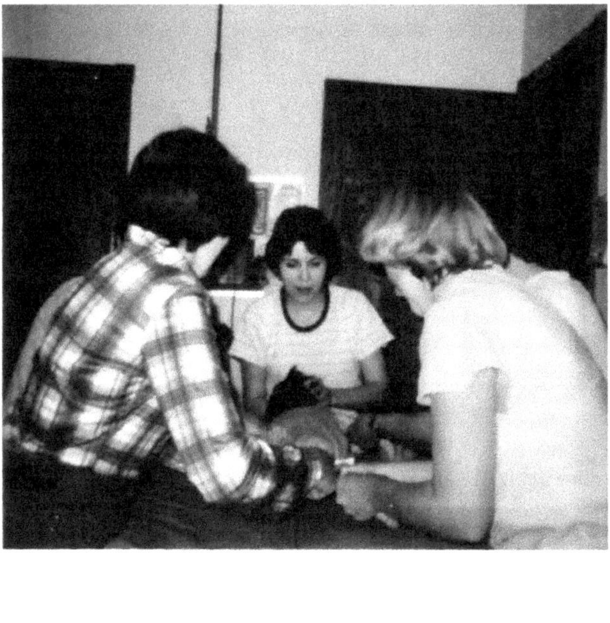

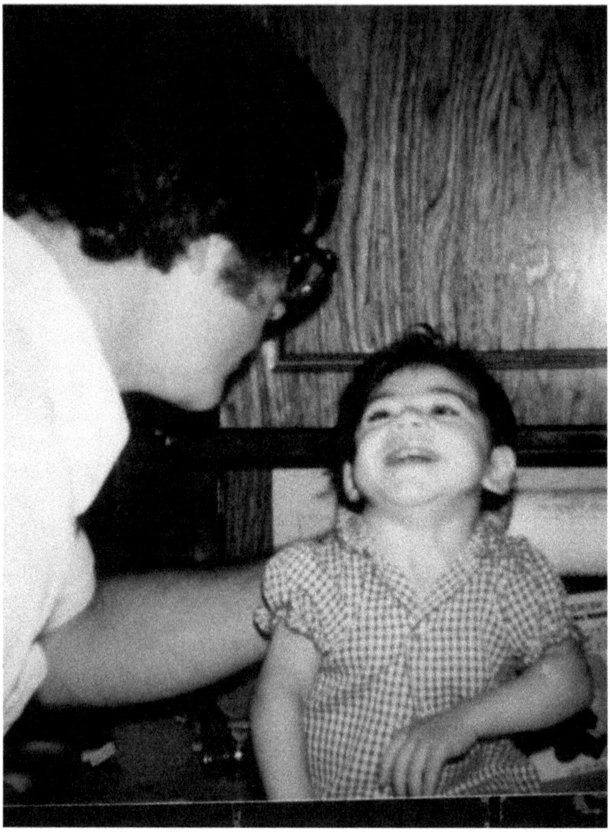

Chapter 10
I AM A PROMISE

"Fight the good fight of the faith. Take hold of the eternal life to which you were called and about which you made the good confession in the presence of many witnesses" (1 Timothy 6:12, ESV).

After another week of classes and much new training, we returned home excited and charged up to start our revised program. On Monday, June 11, I had a meeting for our volunteer patterners. They were very eager to see how much Jan had improved. They, too, were ready to fight the battle again and were equally impressed with the results we'd gotten in our three months of hard work.

On the new program, we no longer needed to use the "light table" as frequently. Jan now saw well enough to notice her toys and what was going on around her. We continued the five hundred watts of lights flashing simultaneously with the introduction of tastes and smells. Because Jan's sense of feel was still not normal, we introduced tactile stimulation with more frequency, duration, and intensity. I warmed a wet washcloth in the microwave until it was very warm...I placed another washcloth in ice water until it was very cold, and we bathed Jan's arms and legs in one, then followed with the other. This really stimulated her sense of feel. Mine too!

A few weeks after we began the new tactile stimulation program, I took Jan to have one of her childhood vaccinations. The poor nurse looked at Jan's skinny little hips and said, "I can hardly bear to give her a shot. There's just no meat there."

"I know," as I tried to comfort her by explaining that Jan's sense of feel was so damaged that she'd not feel the shot. (She never had before.) This time as soon as Jan was injected, she started to scream. I was both surprised and overjoyed. Our seemingly cruel stimulation program was working. Jan was beginning to see and feel her world.

On our revised program, we masked Jan only seventy times a day, but the time now was increased to a minute and a half. Jan was becoming a pro at masking, too, and no longer fought it. By the end of the masking time, she was breathing very deeply in order to get her oxygen, and we knew this, too, was working.

Every day was divided into seven-minute intervals. I soon "knew" when the timer was getting ready to ring, and I was programed to jump up at the ding of any bell. If I wasn't careful, when the microwave dinged at our house or someone else's, I jumped up to mask Jan.

Once, as I was taking Ben to soccer practice, I took along my trusty timer so that I wouldn't get behind on the masking. I planned to mask her as I watched Ben's practice from the car, but I forgot and left the timer on as we drove. It went off while I was stopped at a traffic light. Without thinking, I pressed the gas pedal and ran the red light. For obvious reasons, I decided I'd better make certain the timer wasn't set while I was driving.

The patterns remained much the same, except our little fighting girl was beginning to enjoy them as long as we sang to her the entire five minutes. The most cherished patterners were those who could lead us in five-minute-long silly songs! Music would become a lifelong joy of Jan's, and it impacted our family greatly.

I have never felt I could carry a tune, so I learned to resort to the tape player on days when no singing patterners could be found. Along this time, Bill and Glory Gaither wrote a song for their kids and recorded it, "I Am a Promise." The first time I heard it, I fell in love with it. *"I am a promise / I am a possibility / I am a promise to be anything God wants me to be"* (Copyright: © 1975 by William J. Gaither). It became Jan's theme song. What a joy. If you've never heard it, you can still find it online. It impacted my life so much that I wrote the Gaithers a letter thanking them. I still have the sweet letter that I received back from Gloria Gaither.

From then on, music was vital in Jan's life and ours. It either played or was sung with each pattern and continued as Jan took trips down the inclined plane. As long as we clapped and cheered or sang for Jan, she'd slowly slide to the bottom.

So much wonderful change in Jan. And a new delightful device was introduced at this time called the gravitational device. We built a wooden frame and sewed a muslin cloth sling that would support Jan in a prone position within this frame. We added grommets around the edges of the muslin and heavy-duty springs hooked in them. The other end of the springs was attached to the overhead wooden canopy. When we suspended Jan in the sling, turned on her music, and cheered her on, she had the wonderful opportunity to experience freedom of movement (without the problems of gravity) for the first time in her life.

Jan loved each session, discovering that any movement she made caused her to bounce and swing. The more we cheered her on, the more she moved and giggled. Soon she was soaring in that device.

It remains one of my sweetest memories—Jan smiling, soaring, and enjoying life—patterners watching, cheering, and enjoying her. We nicknamed this device the "spring turtle" because Jan looked like a little turtle with her head sticking up from the sling. Since it was hard for Jan to hold her head up, too, that provided an additional therapy that strengthened her neck muscles. She was suspended in it one hour a day...divided into four fifteen-minute sessions.

What a joy it was for each of us to see Jan actually having fun. What a return the patterners were seeing on their donated gift of time and love—watching our little promise progress as her personality developed daily before our eyes.

Jan also started a beginning seeing program. Words on fourteen by fourteen inches white cardboard written in red/orange fluorescent markers were introduced. We made the cards. I found a source that would cut multiple cards for me, and the patterners helped print the words. These bright words were introduced in a darkened room with a spotlight on each card. We did eight sessions a day, with five words each session.

This was followed by "floor time." We were more aggressive with our "floor time" now, having been given distances Jan had to move before she could get up. Sometimes an ice cube to the foot moved her along quickly. Other times cheering and clapping did the trick. "Floor time" was always followed by many praises and hugs and kisses. And Jan did begin to move. For some reason, she went backwards instead of forward, but the important thing was she was moving.

By June 30, after nineteen days on the new program, many improvements in Jan were readily apparent. She had run fever only once in those nineteen days. We were still slowly decreasing her seizure medication, and her seizures had lessened considerably. She was moving more and had learned to get off the light table, so we had to watch her very closely. This all from a little girl who was almost comatose only five months before. The summer flew by with a flurry of activity and work.

Soon it was time for our return visit to the Institute. Mike had already used all of his vacation time, so for this trip, our pastor's wife, Phyllis, agreed to go with Jan and me. Phyllis had never flown before and was a bit nervous about our flight. I, on the other hand, had never found my way around in a strange city (that was always Mike's department), so I promised to reassure her in flight if she'd do the driving in Philadelphia. (In case I didn't reassure her enough, she also took Dramamine!) We were quite the team.

As always, it was a joy to arrive at The Institutes once again. Being reunited with what was like a second family was one of the things I looked forward to most. How exciting to see some children begin to take their first steps, children who'd never walked and were never supposed to walk. We cheered with those parents, not only for them but for the children and for the staff of the Institute. Children began to crawl who'd never crawled, and some began to read who'd never read. Some began to see well enough to read after they'd been exposed to the light table. Post-brain-damaged days, all of us parents had taken a lot for granted—like crawling, walking, talking, and seeing. We all learned so many amazing things. Who knew the incredible dexterity it took to put the thumb and index finger together to pick up a dime? I also learned a new level of once-taken-for-granted things to be forever thankful for.

Jan's major improvement was in her disposition. She wasn't crawling or using her hands, but she was definitely responding and developing a wonderful personality. This time her chest had increased by 0.8 centimeters. A normal child in the same length of time would average a 0.5 change. Her head size increased also by 0.8 centimeters. An average child's head would have increased by 0.3 centimeters. Her head had grown two-and-a-half times faster than a normal child's head would have averaged in that period of time. That meant her brain was growing. We were thrilled. Again, after a strenuous week of lectures and training, we were ready for our next new program. (The lectures were done by incredible people—people like Linus Pauling, who was an American Nobel Prize-winning chemist. The research he'd done on vitamin C helped our kids greatly.)

Phyllis and I had a tiring but wonderful week. We only were lost a couple of times and considered ourselves a successful duo. (This took place before cell phones and navigational devices too! We read a paper map!) But we weren't home yet; we still had the flight! Phyllis took her Dramamine, and we set off for the last leg of our journey.

We were to have a brief layover in Kansas City and arrive in Oklahoma City by midafternoon. Approaching Kansas City, we encountered extreme turbulence. I'd given Jan a crushed-up Dramamine so she didn't throw up. I'd not taken one, and as I braced both feet against the seat in front of me, I held a throw-up bag in one hand and hugged Jan as tightly as I could with the other.

It felt as if the plane was a giant frisbee being thrown upward and slammed downward. The pilot kept attempting to land...but had such difficulty that he finally came on the intercom to tell us, "Ladies and gentlemen, we are experiencing some difficulties."

"No kidding!"

Half the people on the plane were using their little throw-up bags, all but Phyllis, who had faithfully taken her Dramamine! The stewardesses struggled to keep their balance as they made rounds with trash bags to pick up our "little bags" and pass out new ones. Finally, they were throwing up also and had to be seated. Phyllis and I really thought a crash was imminent. We prayed together, but we were still both strangely at peace as we trusted God with the outcome.

That storm never allowed our plane to touch down in Kansas City, and we were forced to detour to a Wichita airport. Never had God's green earth looked so wonderful. As our entire group deplaned, one had only to look into each pale face, some brows beaded with sweat, other people still crying, to know that we had been through a terribly frightening experience. And to think, I was the one who had assured Phyllis that flying was "no sweat"!

We called Mike and Phyllis' husband, Jack, from a pay phone to tell them we wouldn't be on our flight but would be delayed. We finally made it home a few hours later, and never had home and family looked so wonderful! The next morning, my body was sore all over from the tense situation we'd been in, and I felt physically sick. Phyllis did too.

But a few days later, I held a meeting for my patterners and once again eagerly shared Jan's progress report. They were always excited to hear about Jan's improvements. I gave God the glory for what we'd been able to accomplish and thanked each one of them for their wonderful support. It would be six months this time, instead of three, before we'd return to the Institute, and as usual, we had our work cut out for us. We were a team working together with a common bond—Jan. Someone suggested ordering matching T-shirts. We decided to call ourselves Jan's Clan and ordered red shirts with bold white letters that proclaimed Jan's Clan. When they arrived, even brother Ben proudly wore his to first grade!

There were many new changes to our program. Jan's masking was reduced to fifty-two times a day but increased in time to two minutes each. We continued with the patterns but only needed to do six a day. Our time on the light table decreased to ten two-minute sessions a day. Jan was blind when we started the program. The "light table" restored the blindness that was caused by the brain damage itself, but there had been permanent damage to Jan's optic nerve, and nothing could restore that. She was able to see at close range, and the bigger and brighter, the better. We were told that if intellectually she was able to read, the words would have to be several inches tall for her to see them.

The beginning seeing program changed significantly. This part of the program introduced not only ten by ten inches bright, bold shapes on a fourteen by fourteen inches white background of cardboard but fluorescent red dots, one and a quarter inches in diameter (one to one hundred), and additional reading words still printed in fluorescent paint. The room was still darkened during these sessions, and a spotlight was placed on each homemade card. We were giving Jan every possible advantage to help her see and feel her world.

Jan saw five cards at each session, for a total of eight sessions a day. Two of the cards were shapes (square, triangle, etc.), one card was a dot card, and two cards had words. She saw a total of forty cards a day: sixteen shapes, sixteen words, and eight cards—each having different numbers of dots. The dots were quarter-sized florescent red stickers, and as she saw them, the number would be called out—two or five or ten, etc.—however many dots there were. Each day we added four new shapes, two new dots, and four new words, and we retired four old shapes, two old dots, and four old words. Each card was held up for one to three seconds.

This became something that Jan thoroughly enjoyed—many times, laughing at the same word or picture. An example is one of her favorite words with a picture was "Ring-Necked Pheasant." Of course, what cracked her up cracked us up, so we spent a lot of time laughing as we showed the pictures. We showed her common everyday things, too, that if she were normal intellectually, she would learn easily. (For example, pictures of bananas, apples, eyeglasses, toothpaste, sun, moon, etc.)

We continued with the "Spring Turtle" (four fifteen-minute sessions a day) and the hot and cold stimulation. In addition, we added rubbing Jan down with a vegetable brush (yes, I did say vegetable brush) and a Teflon pad. We rubbed her enough to redden her skin slightly. Since her sense of feel was not normal, the rubbing seemed to feel good to her. I often wondered what people thought the first time they visited our unconventional program. It must have been rather shocking!

Our major new addition to the program was respiratory patterning. We needed an electric metronome and a respiratory jacket to put it into effect. I made the jacket from an institute pattern, making it from muslin and lining it with batting and quilting it to make it strong. It came together in the front very much like a vest would, except that where buttons and buttonholes would have been, there were long straps. The straps crisscrossed and had a dowel through pockets at the end of each strap.

The respiratory patterning took two people in addition to Jan. Jan was placed on her back on the patterning table, and a person was seated on either side of her. When each of us pulled, the jacket tightened around Jan's chest, forcing the air out of her lungs. Jan was patterned at thirty respirations per minute—two beats of the metronome for inhaling and three beats for expiring. The metronome setting was at one hundred fifty. Our goal with this procedure was to help improve Jan's circulation and hopefully decrease some of her tightness. It also gave Jan's brain the information of "this is how breathing correctly feels."

There was only one problem: I had no sense of rhythm. I couldn't follow the beat of the metronome. Since the timing was critical, I had to make certain the second person working with me had rhythm so I could follow their lead. Choir members from our church were great at this! We were to build up our sessions until we were doing respiratory patterning three hours a day. I hoped that this would also retrain my brain, but I still have no sense of rhythm!

In my records, I find this note:

October 28. Jan is twenty-two months old—responds well...cries when she isn't getting her way...or getting fed when she wants it. Laughs at her words and pictures...goes down the inclined plane fairly well...adores praise. Laughs out loud...almost demands entertainment during respiratory patterning...does not like to eat for anyone but me.

God's Grace Keeping Pace

I learned that truly, with God, all things were/are possible. My part was to keep placing all my hard places into His skilled hands and then look for His provision. Let's keep looking for His glimpses of grace—they are always present when we give it all to Him.

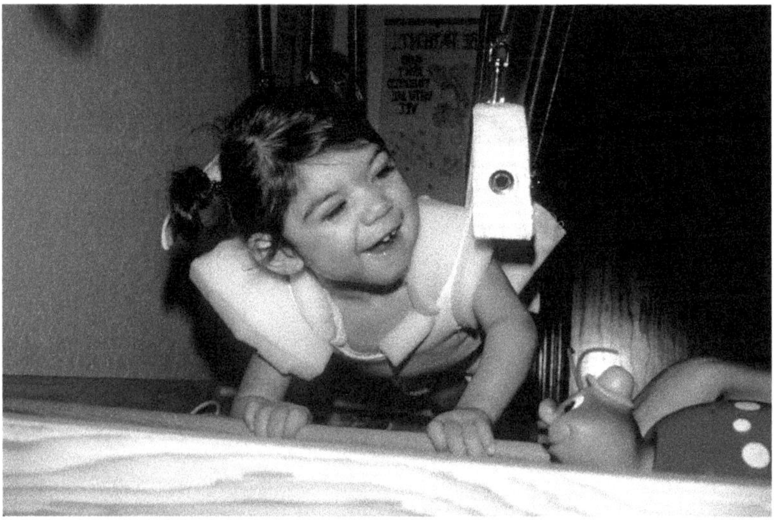

Chapter 11
THERE WAS JESUS

"It is the glory of God to conceal a matter, But the glory of kings is to search out a matter" (Proverbs 25:2, NKJV).

1980

The days turned into weeks and the weeks into months, and before I knew it, Christmas was upon us once again. How different this Christmas would be from the last one! Even Ben was excited over the changes in his little sister. As we decorated the Christmas tree, Ben showed Jan each ornament before he placed it on the tree. He was such a sweet brother.

Most of our ornaments have special meanings or memories, and Ben had helped pick out many of them. He wanted Jan to see his favorite ones. As he showed her a little plastic matchbox ornament, Jan opened her mouth wide. (That was how she "told" me she wanted to eat.) For some reason, Ben shoved the ornament into her mouth. Jan clamped down on it and wouldn't let go.

Ben screamed, "Mom, mom, Jan's eating my ornament, and she won't let go." Turning around, I saw a frightened little girl with a resin matchbox, housing a little mouse, clinched tightly between her few baby teeth. Only the mouse protruded from her mouth! I retrieved it (the mouse) only when Jan started to scream, scared by this thing she couldn't eat. I still love hanging that little Christmas ornament on my Christmas tree fortysomething years later!

Jan's Clan

As the holiday approached, one of my patterners suggested that we all wear our Jan Clan shirts and set aside a December day to have a cookie exchange. That way, all of our patterners could converge at the same time and meet each other. And I could dress Jan up in her Christmas dress and celebrate together the blessings we'd all been privileged to be a part of. It was a wonderful idea and a wonderful new tradition to add to our lives—one that I've continued off and on for over forty years.

No, Jan wouldn't be able to pull the ornaments off the Christmas tree as Ben had at two years of age, but she exuded love to all who knew her. She wouldn't be able to rip the wrapping paper off her presents, but this year she would enjoy Christmas, and so could we. Jan was seeing and feeling her world (including tree ornaments and brother and patterners). My, the things I'd learned to be thankful for. I'd even buy a doll this year. I just had to find one that made noise because Jan had learned to adore silly sounds, encouraged also by us ladies singing loudly to her.

Christmas came and went, and we continued our routine. A new year dawned, and still, we continued our daily routine, but with extra celebration because January 1 Jan turned two. Happy birthday, Jan. That morning as I opened my Bible, my scripture for the day was Isaiah 26:4 (NKJV), "Trust in the Lord forever, For in Yah, the Lord, is everlasting strength." Amen!

Jan was slowly improving, but she still didn't sleep well. By now, we'd been on the program for almost a year, and I really felt the strain. The program moved at such a fast rate each day; every second of my time was taken. I still cooked a full dinner each evening (farm girls raised in the fifties just do that) and sewed occasionally in ten minutes increments. I expected too much of myself, but I kept pushing my body. My sweet friend, Gay, tells me that on Sunday mornings, when I'd place Jan in our church nursery, I'd sit down in her Sunday school class and soon drop my head and go soundly to sleep. She'd teach the class; people would share, and I'd sleep through most of it. I don't remember that, but it was one time that I could relax, knowing that Jan was well taken care of.

In the midst of this physical strain, my emotions were affected too. I longed to have a normal life again. I looked at Mike and let little seeds of resentment grow. This was the height of the oil boom, and he was an oil executive. Even though his day had many pressures, in my mind, if I'm honest, I felt jealous that he could walk out the door every morning at 7:00 a.m. into a different world. I had no such opportunity. My world remained the same twenty-four hours a day. He was wined and dined each day by salesmen. He worked out at a health club three days a week, and the company provided a club membership so that business could also be conducted on the golf course. His life (in my mind) had changed very little, which, of course, wasn't true.

Recalling that non-helpful clinic counselor's words about how many marriages with handicapped children end in divorce, I knew I couldn't let my attitude fester. Both Mike and I were very committed to our marriage, and we'd always had a good relationship. My attitude of resentment was wrong, and I felt convicted about it.

I also knew that when a marriage gets into trouble, the "infection" that causes the breakup begins by nursing one little hurt and then another.

I couldn't let my irritation and resentment continue, and I prayed a very "serious" prayer that went something like this, "Help me, Lord. I know my attitude towards Mike isn't right. Would You change him—and bring his ego down a few notches—then my attitude can be better." Can you believe I prayed that? I already had the "answer" to my situation, or so I thought!

My parents seldom argued, and I wasn't an arguer either. I tended to keep things to myself, so Mike didn't know about my attitude. Nevertheless, it was brewing in the confines of my heart even though it hadn't yet surfaced. Did you notice I was the one with the attitude problem, but I was praying for the change to be in Mike? As God, through His Holy Spirit, began to teach me, I was in for a rude awakening. God took me to the love chapter first.

> Love is very patient and kind, never jealous or envious, never boastful or proud, never haughty or selfish or rude. Love does not demand its own way. It is not irritable or touchy. It does not hold grudges and will hardly even notice when others do it wrong. It is never glad about injustice, but rejoices whenever truth wins out.
>
> 1 Corinthians 13:4–6 (TLB)

He (The Holy Spirit) didn't stop there either. He took me to scriptures that reminded me that I was to love my husband and respect him and obey him (1 Peter 3:1–3 and Colossians 3:18). And I love how the Amplified Bible puts it, "Wives, be subject (be submissive and adapt yourselves) to your own husbands as [a service] to the Lord" (Ephesians 5:22, AMP). God let me know that Mike's walk with Him was His business—*my* walk and *my* heart needed to be my concern. *Ouch.*

I typed several copies of the love chapter on index cards—substituting my name in the place of love—I prayed it and read it repeatedly: "Pam is patient and kind toward Mike, Pam does not demand her own way, Pam will hardly even notice when others do it wrong, Pam does not hold grudges." I placed my typed scripture in places where I'd read it often. God taught me that love was a choice. My resentful feelings hadn't yet changed when I chose to love Mike based on God's definition of love. God's kind of love doesn't leave room for resentment. If you want to strengthen any relationship, this is such a powerful scripture to pray and put into action. It changes us because love truly is an action.

When I made the choice to be obedient to God and His Word rather than focus on my negative feelings and resentments, when I refused to let bitterness or jealousy take up permanent residence in my heart, God took away my resentment and changed my attitude. It was a wonderful lesson I very much needed to learn—God's Word should always, always trump our destructive feelings…and it will if we choose to focus on His truth!

With that tool in my navigating-life God's way box, I was once again able to focus on being thankful for Mike and all of the many good qualities I saw in him daily. The enemy of my soul would have loved to destroy our marriage.

Again, dear reader, printing out that love chapter and placing my name in it and living it out with God's help was one of the best tools I ever added to my toolbox of overcoming.

Whatever God told me to do in His Word (and love was one of the key things He has told us all to do), if I was willing to obey Him, He'd restore the feelings that needed to be within me. He was teaching me so much. Truly nothing was impossible with Him. How wonderful walking according to His Word was.

I was healed of that attitude problem, but my fatigue continued. God, our mighty Comforter, knew I desperately needed encouragement. I noticed something strange occurring. Every night, as many times as I'd get up with Jan, at some point, I'd look over at the digital clock, and the time would be 4:44 a.m. Without fail, when I walked into my bedroom after the patterners left in the afternoon, the clock would read 4:44 p.m. I called to get an airline schedule for my mom to return for a visit—the flight number was 444. I went to church, and we sang hymn number 444. A friend started a new Christian business, and the telephone number was 722–7444. I picked up a couple of things at the grocery store—my bill was $4.44. This continued until I definitely knew it was more than a coincidence.

I mentioned it to my patterners, and one of them told me that her husband (who was in our church) taught on the significance of numbers in the Bible at a nearby college. She suggested that I ask him about my strange reoccurring 444. The next time I saw him at church, I shared my story and asked if he had any insight. He told me about an Arabic numbering system that I could use to find the numerical value of a word. A's value is six, B's value is twelve, C's equals eighteen, D equals twenty-four, etc., the value of each letter increasing by six.

I still have the notebook where I did this calculation. I wrote down the alphabet and assigned the number values to the each of the letters. Among my first words to total was Jesus. I was astounded. Jesus added up to 444, and so did Messiah. It was a precious discovery and one I believe God used to remind me that He was with me every step of the way, no matter where I was. This was such an amazing comfort to my heart! My Heavenly Father, Creator of the Universe, King of kings, had showed me He was with me not only during the long nights but when I went to the grocery store, when I talked on the telephone, and when I went to church. He said in His Word He'd never leave me or forsake me, and He showed me that very clearly.

In the years that have followed, many times when I've felt despair, from seemingly nowhere, 444 still pops up. Sometimes it's on a license tag on the vehicle in front of me, sometimes on a billboard, but always it is a comfort as He reminds me, "Pam, I'm still walking with you." I could've never imagined that God would do something like that to encourage me, but there is a reason He is called the God of all Comfort. He is amazingly faithful.

High Temperatures

Jan didn't make it through the winter without getting sick. She became congested not long after her birthday and, by January 16, was running a temperature of 105°F. On top of that, I had an abscessed tooth. It took several days for the two of us to get back to normal, and then it was back to business as usual. Three weeks later, as we daily did the program, Jan contracted the flu. She ran very high temps, vomited, and had seizures.

By March 8, it was time to leave for the Institute again. Jan was well enough for us to keep our Philadelphia appointment. After her evaluation, we were overjoyed to learn that Jan had once again improved. Her measurements had increased again—her chest by 2.4 centimeters and her head by 0.3 centimeters. *Again, thank You, Lord.*

We'd now been on the program for thirteen months. Jan's weight had increased from thirteen pounds to twenty pounds, and she definitely was not the irritable little girl she had been when we first started. We weren't close to being where a normal two-year-old would be, but at least we were far ahead of where we started. Once again, we trained and learned all that we could and came back inspired to continue our fight against the brain damage. Jan ran a fever the entire time we were at the Institute and continued to do so when we came home. By March 27, I realized she had missed only one day of fever since March 1. She lost two and a half pounds, and after a few nights, her fever went as high as 105.5°F. The doctor couldn't find anything wrong with her, so we decided to slow down for a while.

Toward the end of the first week in April, we slowly began to attempt the new program. It still included the respiratory patterning, six patterns, four spring turtles, ten sessions of words, the usual fifty masks, and much more floor time. Jan hated the floor time. She didn't like being on her tummy, and she didn't like moving, as evidenced by her screaming.

The Accident

On April 28, all of my patterners left after putting in a full day of programing. Ben came home from school, had a snack, and he and a little neighbor boy went out front to play. I looked out the front window just as Ben took an old golf club of Mike's out of the garage and started to practice his swing. I really didn't think about how dangerous that was, but between masking every seven minutes and starting dinner, I kept checking on them. I'd just stepped into the kitchen to stir something on the stove when I heard a loud cry. The front door slammed, and in came Ben with a trail of blood marking everywhere he'd walked.

Running to him, I saw a terrible gash on the edge of his hairline across the left side of his forehead. It was very deep; I felt sick even looking at it. Grabbing a clean wash cloth, I pressed it tightly against the gapping wound to stop the bleeding. I ran to the phone and called our pediatrician's wife, Arlene, who was also a friend and only lived a few blocks away. I screamed into the phone, "Please come quickly, Ben is hurt badly, and I need help." I hung up, and she hurried over.

She helped me load Jan and Ben into her car, and we rushed to her husband's office. Immediately Ben was taken into the examining room. I sat with Jan and waited, telling myself, "Just a few stitches, and Ben will be right out." Dr. Biehler called me into his office shortly and suggested that I call Mike.

"I gave Ben nine shots around the area. Tell Mike to meet us at Baptist Hospital. Ben's skull has a hole knocked in it, and I've already called a neurosurgeon to meet us there. I don't think Ben has any brain damage!"

I was totally stunned. At first, I couldn't comprehend what he'd said, and for a second, I thought he was teasing. Then as his words registered, I knew he wouldn't tease about something like that. At the moment, however, that was easier to believe than the truth! "I don't think he has any brain damage," rang repeatedly in my mind.

Lord, this can't be happening. Please let Ben be all right. Mike met us at the hospital, and Ben was rolled back to surgery. He was in surgery, it seemed, for several hours. Friends from the church and patterners took over Jan's care so that we could stay at the hospital. Mike and I prayed and waited again. This time the report was good. Ben would be all right.

The surgeon was able to reposition the skull back into its proper place. Any pressure placed on it before the bone had time to fuse could cause it to go back down. This was 1980, before staples and other things were available to hold the skull in place. Ben couldn't lay on his stomach to sleep, so he had to be closely watched for several weeks. He came out of the recovery room with a gauze wrapped around his entire head, ending at his neck. He looked like a miniature sheik.

For Ben, the hospital stay was wonderful. For the first time in over two years, he had our undivided attention. I grieved that it took a near tragedy to have time solely for Ben, but I was also very thankful for wonderful friends who made it possible for us to have that time. Ben was in the hospital for four days and wasn't allowed to go back to school for a week. When he did start back on May 7, he couldn't ride the bus or join the other children on the playground for the rest of the school year. No contact sports were allowed for at least a year.

Tough Trip

Again, the time slipped by rapidly, and our next Institute appointment arrived. This time we would take my mom and Ben along. We all flew into Philadelphia on July 26 and prepared for the long week of evaluation and training. We, once again, saw improvements in many areas, but we realized we had a long way to go. The Institute wanted Jan and me to return and live at the Institute for two weeks and let them work with Jan one on one. This was at no extra cost to us (other than my plane fare) and would give them a chance to really concentrate on Jan. How I dreaded that trip. I knew I'd have to go by myself. Mike had no more vacation time left, and Mother needed to stay with Ben.

So only two weeks after returning to Oklahoma, Jan and I left once again for Philadelphia. I had Jan and her medications, stroller, diapers, food, clothes, program records, and very little energy left. We arrived in Philadelphia with Jan running a 103°F temperature. Holding back the tears, I lugged Jan and our belongings off the plane and flagged a cab. That in itself was an accomplishment.

It was late afternoon when Jan and I arrived at The Institutes. We were escorted to our room, which was on the third floor of the massive old mansion, and I do mean massive. Remember, it was built in 1920. It was so big that it had a bowling alley in the basement and had hundreds of rooms.

To my great dismay, I discovered that our air conditioner (which was a window unit) was broken. August in Philadelphia is very hot and humid. Jan still wasn't able to tolerate heat, so I knew we really had a problem. The Institute's solution was to open an office door down the hall and turn on the window unit there to cool our room. This meant I had to leave our bedroom door wide open all night, and with Jan crying most of the night—it was a miserable night.

Jan cried, and I cried. I didn't have a phone in my room, and it was a time before cell phones, so I couldn't phone home! The bathroom was down the hall, and all-night doors slammed in various places in the old building. It was a scary experience for me. I held my Bible close, and I felt the presence of the Lord as I once again cried out for strength.

The two weeks of training crept slowly by. While there, I met a man from Japan that had brought his severely damaged child for the same one-on-one treatment that Jan was receiving. He and I couldn't speak, other than I learned to say hello and goodbye in Japanese, and he learned to say the same in English.

Day in and day out, our paths crossed, and we nodded cordially at each other and tried to speak in "sign language." Several times I watched his little boy for him while he ran a quick errand. One day he came by as I was sitting holding Jan in a little secluded private garden, having a pity party. I was crying because I was homesick, Jan was sick, and I was exhausted and lonely.

I felt so sorry for him because he wanted to help me in some way. His facial expression showed his compassion. He patted me on the back, and all I could say was, "I'm okay," as I nodded my head back and forth. The next day when his son died, I felt such sorrow for him, and all I could do was pat him on the back and shake my head side to side. We couldn't speak each other's language, but that bond of having a brain-damaged child had made us "kindred spirits" for two weeks.

When our two-week stay was over, I could hardly wait to get home. I had valuable new training, but I was so tired I wondered if I'd be able to use it. Jan was still not feeling well. She'd slept very little at the Institute and had run a temperature most of the time we were there. I knew the first thing I had to do was nurse her back to health.

Once we settled in, we started gamma globulin shots and followed that with a week of antibiotic shots. Finally, we were able to start the new program, but I realized that I was gradually losing my stamina, and this time, vitamins and protein drinks weren't building me up.

I found that I could no longer time two minutes on my watch. That was a silly thing, but for almost two years, I'd watched the second hand on my watch every seven minutes all day long. Now, as soon as the second hand went around once, I couldn't remember if that was the first or second time around. It was as if my brain had short-circuited. Mike bought a stopwatch for me, and that solved my problem.

I was determined to continue the program because we were seeing ongoing progress. Jan now enjoyed cartoons on television and delighted in listening to children's tapes. That was huge. Besides Christmas ornaments, this was one of the first things she and Ben could share together.

In November, a company contacted Mike and wanted him to apply for a job in Dallas. It was for a position that was very appealing to Mike. He applied, and by January 2, one day after Jan's third birthday, we put our house on the market as we prepared to move to Dallas. On January 12, Jan and I and a friend flew for the last time to Philadelphia. Our two-year program was over. When the Institute found out we were moving, they told me to take a break, move, and get settled in Dallas before we attempted the program again.

I'd prayed that God would show me when it was time to stop the program. I don't think I could've stopped without the Institute saying, "You have to stop the program until after your move."

At this point, I fully planned to start back afterwards. However, until I had that much-needed break, I didn't realize how close I was to total physical and mental exhaustion. Life had become so abnormal for us; I no longer knew what normal was.

Mike started his new job in Dallas in January. We thought our home would sell quickly, but it didn't. He stayed in a motel in Dallas during the week and flew home every weekend. Finally, by April, we decided we'd buy a home in Dallas and move anyway. On the last day of April, we closed the door for the last time to the home we'd moved into right after my dad's death. I left behind many sweet memories and, with God's help, attempted to leave behind many heartbreaks. Another new journey had begun.

God's Grace Keeping Pace

God, in His grace, taught me so much—things like our feelings are to be processed in light of His Word. We may be tempted to be resentful because life didn't go according to our expectations, but God has called us to praise Him in the midst and love each other. Let's keep looking for His glimpses of grace.

Chapter 12
RESCUE

"To every thing there is a season, and a time to every purpose under the heaven" (Ecclesiastes 3:1, KJV).

Dallas was a totally new lifestyle. Ben had only four weeks of school left when we arrived, and thankfully, that gave him a chance to meet a few children before the school year ended. He was very excited when he found out that our new home was not many blocks from the Dallas Cowboy practice field. They were his favorite football team, and on occasion, we saw the players running in our addition. We were told that a few of them lived nearby, and Ben was always on the lookout for players. He would have worn his Dallas Cowboy jersey every day if I'd let him. I finally bought him another identical one because he loved that jersey so much.

Summer came, and with it, a much-needed break from our old routines. Jan was now a "healthy" three-year-old. In fact, she'd not been sick since December. That was five months minus fever. That was record-breaking. We'd indeed come a long way.

Ben and I explored the area together, and one day as we pushed Jan's little wheelchair around a large TG&Y store, an in-store photographer chased us down to ask if he could take Jan's picture. He told me he had a niece like Jan, and he knew that good pictures were sometimes hard to capture. I allowed him to take her picture, and he took one of the best pictures we've ever had of Jan. I was so pleased.

I decided that the summer would be devoted to family, and I'd wait until fall to return to the program. I was so thankful that Jan was healthy now. I was able to find a couple of babysitters in the neighborhood who were good with her, and I planned outings with Ben. I was still the only one who could feed Jan, so we couldn't be gone more than three hours, but we enjoyed that time, and Ben and I spent most of our days side by side. It was a precious time.

Fall came. I knew I needed to start the program again, but I realized I wasn't ready to go back to such a rigid schedule. As I prayed and discussed it with Mike, we faced the fact that if I ruined my health, all of our futures would be in jeopardy. Much more had to be considered than just Jan.

Jan still had sleep problems, and I lost sleep continually. We decided to start patterning and masking on our own but to hold off actually starting the full-fledged program. The last week in August, right after school started, Ben and a newfound friend passed out copies of the following fliers in our neighborhood:

Hello,

My name is Pam Whitley. I'm your neighbor, and I need your help. I have a little girl whose name is Jan. She is three years old. She suffered brain damage when she was eight days old during open-heart surgery.

We've moved here recently from Oklahoma City. There Jan had seventy "second mommies" working with her. Most of them had worked with Jan for two years—giving one hour a week of their time. During that time, they saw Jan's personality develop into a sweet smiling little girl.

Jan is still totally immobile and needs hours of work before even crawling. It takes five people to pattern Jan (simulate crawling), and that's where I need you. It's very easy, and during the hour you're here, only about fifteen minutes will actually be spent patterning. It's a nice way to meet people, and what could be more rewarding than helping to save another's life.

I will have a coffee Friday, August 28, at 10:00 a.m. If you'd like to see the patterning demonstrated, please come.

Thank you,
Pam Whitley
Patterning Schedule:
Monday, Wednesday, Friday: 9:30–10:30 a.m., 1:00–2:00 p.m.

By August 31, we started our abbreviated program with a whole new set of patterners. I also found that there was a handicapped program available for three-year-olds in the public school system. I enrolled Jan there, and on Tuesdays and Thursdays, she attended school. I actually had some time to myself. It was wonderful. I could meet Mike occasionally for lunch, something I hadn't been able to do for three years!

The new schedule worked for all of us. Jan continued to be healthy and eat well for me. We were excited when she finally made it to twenty-five pounds. The first thing people commented on when they met her was how happy she was, what a sweet disposition she had, and how healthy she looked. No one could believe that she hadn't always been that way. *Again, thank You, Lord!*

We lived just down the street from Ben's school. I asked to be his homeroom mother. In my heart, I longed to reestablish the relationship that I had with Ben before Jan took all my time days. That would be a start.

The first time I helped with a party, I couldn't find a babysitter, so I took Jan. The others kids stared at her and whispered among themselves. Jan was in her little orange wheelchair and, of course, couldn't walk or talk like other three-year-olds. When she was in new surroundings, she didn't smile much because she was busy listening to all the new sounds. I was afraid the children's reaction made Ben uncomfortable, although maybe it was me that it bothered the most.

I asked the teacher if it'd be possible for Ben's class to have a field trip to our home so that I could explain to them about Jan and tell them why she was different. I wanted them to see what Jan was really like. The teacher thought that was a great idea.

We lived in walking distance of the school, and on the day that the kids came, I began by showing them a scrapbook. They looked at Jan's New Year's Day pictures, her pictures before brain damage, and the ones after. As we patterned Jan, I asked the children to join in the singing and entertainment for the five-minute session. Jan giggled and even tried to sing along, saying, "Ooh, ooh, ooh."

It was amazing to watch those third graders go from being afraid of Jan to fighting over who could push her in her chair and play with her next. I thought if only all people could be educated about others who were different, I suspected the results would be the same. Fear would be gone.

Everything seemed to finally be settling down to normal, at least more normal than life had been in a long time. We found a new church and started to feel at home. A few boxes still sat in the corner of one room that I'd not unpacked, but for some reason, I left them there.

Mike wasn't satisfied with his new job. He told me things that were going on at work that made him uncomfortable. We prayed about the situation. Finally, Mike's prayers turned to Lord, get me out of this mess. Of course, his plan was for someone to offer him a better job. As we know, God doesn't always work the way we expect.

Mike went to work one Monday in October and found a letter on his desk asking for his resignation. We were stunned. That wasn't the answer we were anticipating, but it certainly worked. It quickly got Mike out of the mess. It also was the beginning of a transition in Mike's walk with God. Being fired was a very humbling experience. In the years that followed, when Mike shared his testimony, he said he needed to be humbled, and God knew just how to do it.

Mike had many connections in Oklahoma but few in Texas. He was discouraged and decided he didn't want to stay in Texas but wanted to go back "home." Within two days, he'd found a new job in Oklahoma, and we'd put our Texas home up for sale. We'd lived there only six months. Our home in Oklahoma had sold four months earlier, so we had to find another place to live.

We knew we wanted to buy in the same school system that Ben had previously attended, so that left us only four houses to choose from. By December, we'd moved. The new home we found was perfect for us, and it was built on a lot we'd considered purchasing the year before we'd moved to Dallas. Knowing our situation with Jan and that we'd moved only a few months before, Mike's new boss hired a sweet lady to help me unpack so that we'd be ready for Christmas. I knew God was in control, and it was wonderful to be back among our old friends.

God Grace Keeping Pace

I found that God met me in unexpected places—like TG&Y for a treasured picture of Ben and Jan. He taught me to humble myself and ask for help along my journey and to accept others' help too. He seemed to emphasize that I wasn't to go back to my independent and self-sufficient ways. Let's keep looking for His glimpses of grace.

Chapter 13
CRY OUT TO JESUS

"Jesus did not promise to change the circumstances around us. He promised great peace and pure joy to those who would learn to believe that God actually controls all things" (Corrie ten Boom).

Another Christmas came and went. January 1 was once again cause for great celebration. Jan, who wasn't supposed to live to be three, had made it to her fourth birthday. Ben blew her candles out on her cake for her, and she giggled with delight as we sang happy birthday. She wasn't at all impressed with the cake since her diet was still sugar-free. She promptly spit it out, making funny faces to show her dislike. I wish I reacted that way to sweets!

By now, we'd been off the program for a full year, and I realized that I'd never go back on it. I was thankful for the two years that we'd done it, but in order for Jan to have a chance of getting well (we did see kids get well on the program), we realized that we were looking at many years of the grinding schedule and then there were no guarantees. Even if physically and emotionally I could keep up the pace, these were Ben's growing up years too. I wanted his memories to be more than years and years of therapy. Also, the program was very stressful for Jan, and given the diagnosis of her short life expectancy,

I wasn't sure it was fair to her. She was happy, now, just as she was. It was a hard decision, but one that we had to make…no more program.

I enrolled Jan in a school for handicapped children provided by the public school system, and our lives took on another new normal. The days and weeks flew by, and abnormal became my norm. I seldom thought about how different Jan was.

One evening, Mike and I attended a Sunday school party. I was seated between two proud new mothers. Their children were each about eighteen months old. They began to talk with one another about all of the cute things their children were doing and saying, leaning over me to communicate with one another. I knew they never thought about Jan and wouldn't have done anything to hurt me, but I could hardly contain my tears. It made me realize just how handicapped Jan was. I wanted to crawl under the table and sob. I continued to smile and listen to their antidotes, but my heart cried out, "God, why does it have to be so hard?"

Finally, at home, in the solitude of the night, I cried and cried. When I'd finished my little pity party, I slipped quietly into bed. Mike was already asleep. As I lay my head on my pillow, from within, I heard a poem. I got up and quickly wrote down the thoughts that had formed in my mind:

The Child Who Was

The child who was would now walk and talk and get into messes and crumble her cookies and mess up her dresses. The child who was would now tumble out of bed for cartoons and kisses and run to meet daddy and stack

> mommy's dishes. The child who was would now fight with her brother and play with the neighbor kids and say, "Mommy, I love you." The child who is has deep within the child who was, and in my mind, somedays I see her skip and play. The child who is is a special gift from God, and though she doesn't know that there is a child who was, she is happy right where she is. Thank You, God, for the child who is and for that glorious day that she will meet You, Lord, face to face, and the image in my mind of the child who was will be a reality.

I felt God had given me that poem to encourage me, and even though it made me cry to read it, it also gave me peace. Jan would, indeed, one day be whole, and this life, compared to eternity, was not even an inch on the scale of time. Yes, we'd all make it, including me. *Again, thank You, Lord, for your faithfulness.*

More Changes

Before I knew it, another year had come and gone, and it had been a year of good health for Jan too. Another birthday, another praise, and thanksgiving to God. Jan was now five, and the little girl that was supposed to die of pneumonia by the time she was three had not ever had it.

I soon found that the year would hold many changes for our family. Mike had the opportunity to start his own business. In February of that year, Whitley Engineering was born. Because of Jan's preexisting condition, our new insurance company wouldn't insure her for six months. They also wouldn't provide coverage for the extra physical therapy Jan was receiving. Jan had been relatively healthy for the past two years, so we weren't too concerned about the six months with no insurance for Jan.

Time for Me

Jan was going to school full days now, and I had more time for myself. I set new goals. One was to be in a Bible study. During the two years of program, several of my patterners were in Bible studies, many times sharing the exciting lessons they were learning. I'd dreamed of the time that I, too, could be in a ladies' Bible study. It was something I'd taken totally for granted before Jan was born. Now I knew it was a privilege.

Another goal I had for the year was to visit Kenneth Hagin's Bible school, Rhema. Two things put that desire there. God had given me Isaiah chapter 42 when Jan was six months old, and I hadn't given up on Jan's being healed. I'd read several of Brother Hagin's books on healing. What impressed me about his teaching was how grounded in the Word it was. I'd learned a lot from reading His books, but more than that, his books made me search the Bible for myself.

The other thing that increased my desire to visit Rhema was the prayer that the evangelist had prayed when we attended the healing service, "For these parents, I pray wisdom." I wouldn't leave any stone unturned for this little girl that I loved so much. I knew Mike's schedule was far too hectic for him to go with me, and Jan and I couldn't go alone. I discussed this desire with no one but Mike and God.

God, if it is Your will for me to go to Rhema, will You work it out?

It wasn't but a couple of weeks until my friend, Gay, called, saying, "I know you don't know my sister, Fran, but she had been praying for you since Jan was born. She wants to talk to you about something God has laid on her heart."

I told her that I'd be happy to visit with her sweet sister.

Fran called and said, "A minister named Kenneth Hagin has a class on healing at his Bible College in Tulsa. It is open to anyone who has sickness in their family. I don't know if you are familiar with his ministry or not, but would you and Jan be interested in going to one of the classes with me?" *Wow!*

I was totally elated and told her about my prayer. We made plans to go. My mom was visiting, so she took care of Ben's schedule. Everything worked out perfectly.

I spent several days prior to going praying and studying my Bible. I wanted to see what He wanted me to see and hear what He wanted me to hear. I didn't want to close any door that He might choose to open for Jan, but I also didn't want to be steered in a wrong direction either. *God, help my faith to be totally rooted in You and Your word, not a man nor a denomination nor my own preconceived notion of who You are.*

Rhema Bible College is located in Broken Arrow, Oklahoma, a small town southeast of Tulsa. It's about a two-hour drive from Oklahoma City. Fran and I left very early, arriving in time for the morning healing class. The young woman teaching the class that morning began by leading us in songs of praise. She had a beautiful voice, and her spirit was humble and sweet. I felt totally at ease. She said, "We just want to spend some time exalting the Lord."

But Lord, I don't know how to exalt You. Please, teach me.

Immediately the young woman said, "There may be some of you who do not know how to exalt the Lord. Just close your eyes and sing your praise to Jesus. Think only on Him and what He has done for you. He'd have died on the cross for you had you been the only one.

He is worthy to be praised. Tune out the people around you, tune out your circumstances, and think only on Jesus."

Until that moment, I'd not really known how to praise God. Sitting in church every Sunday for years, I'd sung traditional songs, but I'd not really praised. As I focused totally on Him and tuned out everything around me, tears slipped down my cheeks, and I couldn't help but raise my hands in praise to my Savior. I'd never done that in my denomination, but it came naturally as I focused on Him and praised Him. What a wonderful experience, singing my praise to my Jesus. God truly does inhabit the praises of His people; I felt His presence strongly.

After the praise, the teaching began. We studied the scriptures in depth. Jesus was becoming so real to me that I could almost feel the excitement in the streets of Jerusalem as He passed by two thousand years before. The scriptures were taking on new life before my eyes, and I knew that my walk with God would never be quite the same again.

Later we went into an auditorium for additional teaching. I felt the presence of the Prince of Peace once again, as I had in the chapel at Children's Hospital five years before. I now understood why He told His disciples it was better for Him to go than to stay. His leaving made it possible for Him to walk with me just as He walked with them two thousand years before.

Fran and I learned a lot that week, and we met many wonderful people who loved God with all their hearts. God quickened one particular scripture to me that was life-changing also: "Casting down imaginations, and every high thing that exalteth itself against the knowledge of God and bringing into captivity every thought to the obedience of

Christ" (2 Corinthians 10:5, KJV).

From that Scripture, I learned to stop worrying about many things, things that were only imaginations or what I like to call *what-ifs*. Again, I was so thankful that God had opened the door for me to be fed so richly in His Word. It helped to prepare me for the many trials that still lay ahead.

After my trip to Rhema, I came home with a new hunger to study the Bible. I was shocked at how many Christian words I'd heard and used all of my life that I really didn't fully understand. I began to study grace, redemption, righteousness, sovereignty, and continued to study healing. I never knew how little I knew until I started to eagerly study. I wanted to learn all I could and be used of Him. I realized that only those things done for Jesus would last.

Now to meet my other goal for that year—attend a Bible study. I visited one at my own church and found out it was not really a study. This was a day before there was an abundance of women's studies like the ones we have today. I again prayed, and soon, a friend mentioned that she had found an in-depth Bible study on the south side of town and invited me to go with her. It sounded exactly like what I wanted.

It was a forty-five-minute drive weekly, but it was well worth it. It consisted of a workbook with questions and tapes that corresponded to the workbook. There were about fifteen people in the study. What a blessing those people were. We learned so much from what they shared. I was astonished by their faith and the number of scriptures they had committed to memory. Not only did they mark the scripture in their Bibles, but it was obvious that the scripture marked them.

I still recall one of those lessons over forty years ago. It covered forgiveness and the important role it plays in the life of a believer. It really impacted me. We studied the scriptures on forgiveness first, and then this amazing true story was shared; it impacted me greatly. I'll share it with you:

Called to Forgive

There was a widow named Hannah who had only one child, a daughter. That daughter was a wonderful young woman and was studying to become a missionary. She'd come home from work five days a week, have dinner with Hannah, and then attend her college night class.

One night she never came home from her class. Hannah knew something bad had happened. Unfortunately, it was eventually discovered that her daughter had been murdered. The authorities caught and arrested the man who killed her, held the trial, and the murderer went to prison. Hannah hated him, and that hate became rage as the years passed by. It consumed her.

One Sunday morning, a Gideon preached at her church. He spoke on the importance of forgiveness. "Get rid of all bitterness, rage and anger, brawling and slander, along with every form of malice. Be kind and compassionate to one another, forgiving each other, just as in Christ God forgave you" (Ephesians 4:31–32, NIV).

Hannah was certain God didn't expect her to forgive that man, but she was wrong. She prayed, and God spoke to her heart, "Hannah, you'd better be prepared to never sin again if you don't forgive this man."

Hannah was rather shocked, but she wanted to walk in obedience. She went to the altar and asked the Gideon to pray with her as she poured out her story. She asked God to help her let go of her rage and hate. As a step of faith, she purchased a Gideon Bible from the speaker. She asked him to make sure her daughter's murderer got it. In that Bible, she scribbled these words: "I'm the mother of the girl you murdered. I forgive you, and I love you in the name of Jesus."

Long story short, the speaker was so touched that he personally took the Bible to the Colorado prison where the man was confined. Before it was all over, the murderer came to know Christ. No one had ever told him they loved him. He wrote Hannah, asking for forgiveness, and she wrote him back.

Hannah's story ended with these words, "God is so frugal. When I forgave that man, God moved on his heart, and he became a missionary in a place where my daughter could have never gone." What an amazing God we serve.

Obedience to Him

I learned that obedience to God's word, regardless of how we feel, moves God's hand in mighty ways. I wanted to walk in that kind of obedience.

That Bible study was where God wanted me for that season of time. He wasn't just teaching me how to apply His Word and to pray His Word, but He was showing me that His children were found under many different titles—Baptist, Methodist, Catholic, Church of Christ, Pentecostal—those were all man-made labels that meant nothing. My brother was no less my brother because he worshiped under a different title or in a different way.

What made anyone my brother was that they had accepted Jesus Christ and His work on the cross as their path to heaven. Yes, God was teaching me many things—many things I'd have never learned had I not had a little girl named Jan who couldn't walk, talk, or use her hands. God does work everything to our good when we commit it to

Him, even brain damage.

In the fall, I took a break from my studies because Jan had several infections.

The congestion was making it difficult for her to eat, and she dropped weight. Dr. Biehler gave her a round of shots, and she appeared to get better. But one morning, she slept later than usual. My friend, Ginger, dropped by to check on us. It was almost eleven o'clock, and I told Ginger I was concerned about Jan. She never slept that late.

Ginger went with me to wake Jan up. I turned on the light and saw that Jan was very purple. When I touched her, it was obvious that she had a high temperature. I grabbed her and quickly ran to the sink. I didn't take time to take her temperature because I could tell it was very high—too high. I fanned her and began to run cool water over her in an attempt to lower her fever, at the same time calling Dr. Biehler's office to alert him that we were on our way. We dressed Jan quickly, and Ginger drove us to the doctor's office. Dr. Biehler took one look at Jan and told us to go directly to Baptist Hospital.

Rushing through the traffic, the drive to Baptist Hospital only took about five minutes. Ginger pulled into the emergency entrance, and I jumped out of the car and raced in the door with Jan. She was still purple and very hot. The nurses were expecting us and immediately whisked her away. My hands shook as I filled out the hospital forms. I wondered if Jan would make it this time. It also dawned on me that Jan probably wasn't covered by our insurance yet. At that moment, that was the least of my concerns.

Within minutes, Jan was in a room. She was placed under a mist tent, given an IV, and I watched as it pumped a cocktail of antibiotics into her bloodstream. It didn't take long for her color to return to normal. After a week of those strong antibiotics, Jan was able to come home. We found out the day Jan went in the hospital was her first day of coverage on our new insurance policy. As always, I was amazed at God's hand of protection. *Thank You, Lord. Your timing is always perfect!*

God's Grace Keeping Pace

God continued to send people to walk this journey with me as He continued to equip me with His Word. He was teaching me more and more to keep shaping my worries into prayers. He was truly teaching me I could walk through anything, holding on to His hand. Let's keep looking for His glimpses of grace.

Chapter 14
HOW GREAT IS OUR GOD

"Do not be anxious about anything, but in every situation, by prayer and petition, with thanksgiving, present your requests to God" (Philippians 4:6, NIV).

Jan fully recovered, and before I knew it, January 1 arrived once again—another year, another celebration. Jan turned six. We counted each birthday a miracle, especially this one after our week in the hospital. Each birthday always brought with it a bit of sadness, too, further reminding us of the growing difference between Jan and her peers. I couldn't help but think of the child who was and what she'd be doing if the brain damage hadn't occurred. I never allowed myself to give it more than a passing thought, but year after year, those thoughts did surface, along with the thankfulness of being allowed another year with Jan.

Without realizing it, we developed our own family practices of dealing with our situation with Jan, just as any family does with any child. At six, Jan was still "little Miss Personality," smiling and giggling much of the time. There were certain sounds or words that really got her attention and provoked uncontrollable laughter in her and all of us.

For example, one night, Jan was watching a television series, The Jeffersons. George Jefferson, in the fashion only he could speak, said, "Wizzy, he owes me fifty bucks." For some reason, Jan loved the way that phrase sounded. She laughed so hard she flipped onto her side and still was giggling. So, guess what our family went around saying for the next several years, "He owes me fifty bucks!"

"S" sounds were a whole other story—like sassafras and silly Sally and Susan, Susan, Susan. For some reason, she loved words with "s's," particularly if the "sss-ss" sound was exaggerated. Each week we discovered something new that was hysterically funny for Jan, and we took full advantage of it. One night while driving in the car, Mike thought he was about to get a ticket—that word ticket cracked her up, so we took full advantage of that word for years as well…saying, "Oh no, don't give me a ticket, ticket, ticket." It was rather hysterical to be around our entertaining family, I'm sure.

One day, we were in the car, and I was drinking a Sonic drink. I moved the straw up and down to stir the ice, and it made a loud squeaking sound. Jan giggled in delight. From then on, if we had drinks with straws, we'd have a chorus of squeaking going on. If we only knew, Jan was probably laughing at how ridiculous we all appeared to her as we repeated our silly sounds and phrases over and over and slid our straws in our drinks. I can't wait to find out what she really thought when we're reunited in heaven.

We also developed the habit of "talking" for Jan. One of us would say what we thought Jan would say. One day when Ben was being a bit rebellious, he said, "Mom, it is so stupid sounding, the way you always talk for Jan." Without thinking, he walked over by Jan and said in a small voice on Jan's behalf, "Yeah, you guys always say things for me that I'd never say." It took him a second to realize what he'd done.

We both laughed and laughed.

Then there was the matter of music. Jan loved music, but she was very opinionated about it. If she didn't like it, she started to fuss and looked away from her tape player. (She preferred cartoon-sounding tapes, similar to the voices on *The Fox and the Hound* or *The Little Mermaid.*)

As Ben became interested in music tapes, one day, he proudly brought home Dolly Parton's *Working Nine to Five*. He played it first on Jan's tape player. She looked away from the tape deck and started to fuss loudly. He promptly removed his tape. Sorry, Dolly.

Still, we weren't without our problems. Lack of sleep continued to be one of our biggest challenges. The area of her brain that allowed Jan to relax never healed, but her body still needed sleep. Finally, our doctor placed Jan on a nighttime sedative. It helped, but as she drew drowsy, she stiffened her little body and fought going to sleep. Her cries were still like an infant, only several decibels higher. Since no one could sleep with her screaming, I'd stay up and rock her. This kept her calm until she could fight the sleep no longer. Usually, by midnight, I'd put her to bed and fall wearily into bed myself. Bedtime was something I dreaded. Very seldom did she sleep through the night.

Feeding Jan continued to be another of our big problems too. Mike was still unable to feed her, but the teachers at school were slowly learning. As Ben observed me feed Jan one day, he said, "Poor Jan, no wonder she eats for you. You just shove it down her and don't give her a choice!" Perhaps that was the real reason she ate so well for me.

Feeding her was unquestionably tedious, and few people could do it. I think she choked and coughed so much attempting to eat that it was too scary for people. I was just used to it.

I learned that certain concoctions of food were easier for her to handle than others. It seemed a banana mashed in each feeding helped her to swallow. Chicken, mashed banana, and a veggie seemed a weird combination, but it worked for Jan. She'd always choke and spit and sputter as I fed her, so I learned to put a robe over my clothes and a large bib on her.

One morning I had an early appointment. I realized I could make that appointment if I was dressed and ready to go when Jan's bus picked her up. I got ready, did my hair and makeup, and then threw on my robe. I fed Jan and rushed her out to the bus as soon as it arrived. I hurried back in and grabbed my purse, and as soon as the bus pulled off, I hopped in the car. Thankfully, I quickly glanced in the rear-view mirror at my reflection. I had a tablespoon-sized-wad of Jan's food sitting right on top of my head. Jan had a typical coughing spell while I was feeding her, but I'd not seen where her food went until that glimpse. I laughed so hard because I'd almost arrived at my meeting wearing a big blob, compliments of Jan, on top of my head. That taught me to never leave home without first checking in a mirror.

Since Jan's feedings were every three hours, when she wasn't in school, we were on a structured feeding schedule. Again, Jan was like an infant, so when she was hungry, she was fuzzy. If I needed to run errands, I watched the time and was always home in three hours. That schedule continued for thirteen years. When Jan no longer lived at home, it took me several years to stop checking my watch because that schedule was deeply engrained in my psyche.

The only part of the original program that I continued after stopping the Institute program was Jan's diet and vitamins. I'd increased the quantity but still gave her five to six meals a day, each with plenty of protein. Most meals had frozen cubes of pureed chicken, heated in the microwave, and mashed together with other good-for-you stuff like broccoli, bananas, green beans, and squash. I continued to feed her at least one yogurt a day, and her health remained above average.

However, the cerebral palsy (brain damage to motor controls) increasingly took a toll on her body. She never once in her life was able to feel her face or touch her mouth. And as time went by, her limbs progressively grew tighter and tighter as her wrist twisted and her thumbs pulled inward toward her palm, and her fingers formed a loose fist over her thumb.

She couldn't wear coats or anything that buttoned down the front because her arms weren't flexible enough to go back far enough to put them on. I learned to buy her warm capes or have them crocheted for the winter, and I turned them backwards and buttoned them at the neck. I sewed her knit sweatshirts and pants for her daily clothing. I could move her arms above her head to pull on a sweatshirt but couldn't move them behind her to pull on a shirt sleeve or coat. When limbs aren't used, they gradually waste away. Some form of physical therapy is the only thing to slow that process. I tried to daily stretch her limbs, but sadly I didn't provide nearly enough movement for her.

After we'd stopped the patterning program, I'd taken Jan to a physical therapist three times a week. When Mike started his own business and we'd changed insurance companies, the new policy didn't provide coverage for her physical therapy, and I had to stop the therapy sessions. As handicapped as Jan was, it would've cost a small fortune to provide the extensive therapy she needed. It saddened me to see her condition deteriorate. I'd often seen teenagers with CP and wondered how their limbs became so taunt and drawn. Now I understand.

In the summer, swimming was one therapy that Jan could enjoy, and she certainly needed it. Because she still couldn't tolerate heat, summers were normally very long and difficult, and swimming was about the only thing that Jan could do outside. The coolness of the water kept her body temperature down. We had one problem, where do you take a six-year-old to swim who is in diapers?

We decided we really needed our own pool. We'd put one in the summer before we moved to Dallas, not knowing we'd be moving. Not only did I not know how to swim well, but I was afraid of water. But since one would be so beneficial for Jan and great for Ben, we prayed about it. Amazingly, the value of some old stock unexpectedly increased to the dollar amount of the pool, and we felt we had our answer.

The pool was a great investment in our family's life. For the first time since Jan was born, in the heat of the summer, we all enjoyed something together. Jan dearly loved swimming. I purchased a swim float made especially for handicapped children. It was oblong foam and (for lack of a better description!) shaped like a toilet lid, but it had an oval cut just big enough for Jan's head to fit inside. Velcro closed the opening behind her neck. It was wonderful. It allowed her the freedom to move about by herself. She'd put her toes on the shallow end bottom for a while, and then she'd bring her toes to the surface of the water. She'd paddle contentedly from one end of the pool to the other, and that neck float totally kept her head above the water at all times. It was wonderful.

One day as Mike brought Jan out to swim, holding her on his hip, minus her float, he decided he'd surprise her by jumping directly in instead of walking down the steps of the pool. Jan wasn't the only one he surprised! Hearing a loud splash, I looked around to see Mike and Jan sitting on the pool floor with only the top of Mike's baseball cap above water. (His feet had slipped out from under him.) There they sat, both underwater, Mike with his hat and glasses still on.

Before I could come to their aid, Mike stood up. For a second, we both held our breaths, wondering if Jan would be choked. She gasped, squealed, and began to giggle. She thought it was a fantastic game. If she could have spoken, I think she would have said, "Do it again, Daddy!" What a blessing that pool was to all of us. God truly does supply all of our needs, even a pool if it will help a little girl in need of therapy and a boy and his family in need of fun activity.

By now, Ben was almost eleven. He was becoming involved in more activities. As Jan became heavier and harder for me to lift, it was wonderful that Mike had his own business. (I always have felt that, too, was part of God's provision of grace for us.) When Ben had a dental appointment, guitar lesson, or haircut appointment after school, Mike could normally schedule time at home to keep Jan.

As the months rolled on, Jan continued to grow, but I didn't! I still remained slightly over five foot two, and her care became more difficult. Many things became easier to just forget about than to attempt to do!

Vacations became almost impossible, but we still tried to go to Mississippi once or twice a year. We packed an ice chest filled with food for Jan and looked for places along the way to stop and warm it. The trip took fourteen hours. If we stopped halfway at a motel, Jan didn't sleep and would keep us all awake most of the night. It was easier to drive straight through.

The spring was our favorite time to go to the South. It always brought back sweet memories to me of long walks among flowering crab apple trees, dogwood blossoms, black-eyed Susans, and wild violets. I looked so forward to those trips. I was determined to continue to make them, and Mike was always so gracious to drive us there. That was the only time I got to see my extended family. So early in the spring, we made another one of our Mississippi trips.

I held Jan most of the way. She tired after the first few hours and arched her back and pushed backwards. That was her way of letting me know she'd rather be doing something else. Fourteen hours later, when we finally arrived at my mom's, I had large clear blisters rubbed on my right arm the size of fifty-cent-pieces where Jan had pushed my arm repeatedly into the armrest. My body was so exhausted that I had difficulty getting out of the car. The long night still stretched before me. Jan stayed awake until 4:00 a.m., and by daybreak, both Jan and I were sick. I was disheartened. By the time she and I recovered, it was time for the fourteen-hour drive back to Oklahoma. What a miserable trip!

I loved going home, but I knew we couldn't make the trip again in the same fashion. I prayed, "Lord, You know how much it means to me to go to Mississippi. *Again, thank You, Lord*

Before the next trip, we purchased a full-sized van with a queen-sized bed in the back. It was equipped with a television and VCR, and both Jan and Ben loved to travel after that. Again, thank You, Lord. It seemed with every obstacle, God provided a solution. More and more, I learned to trust Him with all things. The way was not easy, but my burden was light when I turned it over to Him. His grace truly kept pace with our needs.

As the weeks and months sped by, Jan's body continued to grow tighter and tighter. Shortly after her ninth birthday, one day, I noticed Jan holding her left leg in the air as if she was having a spasm. The leg trembled, and Jan cried out in agony. The first time it happened, I thought maybe she'd had a leg cramp, and that would be the end of it, but it began to happen often. I made an appointment with an orthopedic specialist and took her for an exam. X-rays showed that Jan needed to have surgery. Her hamstrings needed to be released behind the knees and in the groin area. This was a major surgery. It would be life-threatening for Jan but had to be done for her comfort. Recovery would be slow, the doctor warned, if Jan survived!

So, in April, reluctantly, Mike and I checked Jan into Children's Hospital. She'd have surgery at daybreak the next morning. I spent most of the night praying and trying to rock Jan to sleep.

I pleaded, "Lord, please don't let Jan suffer. I'd rather You take her, Lord, than for her to suffer."

After the long night, morning finally came. Mike and Ben arrived, and we kissed Jan goodbye as she was taken to surgery. With the heart surgeon on standby in case of cardiac arrest, Jan came through the surgery with no complications.

I expected her to be groggy for the next several hours. I was wrong. She woke up in the recovery room, screaming. She had a cast from her waist to her toes, and a wide bar between her legs held her legs far apart. She was in misery and very angry about whatever had happened to her while she slept. I'm sure she wondered what she had done to deserve such treatment. My poor little girl!

The whole day was a nightmare for Jan and for us. Since crying still brought Jan's temperature up, we had to do whatever it took to keep her calm. Finally, with three people working with her, one sponging her face and chest with a cool cloth, the second one fanning her, and the third one singing to her, we were able to calm her for short periods of time.

The surgeon made his rounds later in the day. Taking one look at me and my frazzled nerves, he said, "Mom, I know it's awfully hard to see Jan crying so much, but actually, it is the best thing she could be doing. After surgery, in kids like her, we really worry about pneumonia. Her crying is helping to keep her lungs strong and clear!"

And to think, I felt God had let me down because it seemed He'd not answered my prayer (the one about not letting Jan suffer). So much of the time, my sincere prayers were not in her best interest. Would I ever learn that He always knew what was best? Jan's crying was literally saving her life.

Bedtime came, and Mike offered to stay the night with Jan and me. I sent him home with Ben, knowing that it had been an upsetting and difficult day for both of them. After they left, I really thought about the long night that stretched ahead. I'd been awake for almost thirty-six stress-filled hours, and I was exhausted.

Lord, please send someone to stay with us tonight. I don't think I can make it by myself. I knew I had to have rest because I was weak and could barely stand. Looking at the clock, I realized it was already past 10:00 p.m.

Who am I kidding? No one is going to come this late at night.

I was surprised when the phone rang. As I answered, I heard the sweet voice of my neighbor, Kay. "Pam, I was just thinking about you and Jan. Don't you need someone to stay with you tonight?" I was too choked up to speak, but my sobs answered her question.

She said, "I'll be there as soon as possible." What a godsend Kay was that night.

As I hung up the phone, I thought, *Oh, precious Lord, You are so faithful. Thank You, thank You.* The blessing of that answered prayer gave me energy for the days that followed.

After a week in the hospital, we brought Jan home. She was still one miserable little girl. We rented a hospital bed and placed it in our kitchen. We also rented an adult reclining wheelchair. The only time Jan was not fussing was when I was rolling her outside in that wheelchair, and the bumper path I took, the more she enjoyed it. What a sight we were. Every morning by 9:00 a.m., we were cruising up and down the neighborhood streets. (I'm sure the rental chair was practically worn out when we returned it.)

An inquisitive gentleman who observed one of our morning marathons said, "Wow, she must have had one doozie of a wreck."

I laughed, thinking, *Mr., you don't know the half of it!*

The cast was supposed to stay on for six weeks. After three weeks of Jan crying most of the time, I thought I could stand no more. For all I knew, she could have bed sores inside the cast. I talked to the doctor's office several times, but finally, I called with Jan in the room near the phone. I wanted to make certain they understood what we were going through. After hearing her screams, they asked how soon I could bring her to his office. "Believe me, I can be there very quickly!"

Taking the cast off three weeks early, he found the inside of the cast totally saturated with moisture. Jan had perspired profusely each time she cried. It would take several weeks for our lives to get back to normal.

Jan recovered in time to go back to school by fall, and I was ready for a break too. I enrolled for my second year of Bible Study Fellowship. It was another of the Bible studies that my patterners had shared about years before. The discipline and scriptures that I learned there helped prepare me not only for the many difficult days that yet lay ahead and also laid the foundation for a future ministry that I never expected.

God's Grace Keeping Pace

I was truly learning I could trust Him in all things. He cared, He saw, He knew, and He was at work in the midst, and I could trust His heart. Let's keep looking for glimpses of His grace even when our minds don't understand the "hows or the whys" of what we are going through.

Chapter 15
SEND THE LIGHT

"For I received from the Lord what I also passed on to you" (1 Corinthians 11:23a, NIV).

In the early days of walking through our painful situation with Jan, a cousin sent me a wonderful letter—another important grace to my life. In it, she shared the fascinating story of Joseph as she encouraged me to keep walking by faith. I'd read Joseph's story many times, but never through eyes of pain. Her letter ministered to me mightily and gave me needed insight.

Talk about someone's life that didn't turn out like they'd planned; Joseph was the poster child for disappointment and betrayal. His brothers hated him and sold him into slavery. While a servant, he was falsely accused of rape and imprisoned. He spent years and years in hardship, but God watched over Him each step of the way as Joseph trusted God's hand. Joseph chose not to walk in self-pity. He didn't blame others or God for his plight. Because of his choices, his obedient heart benefited thousands upon thousands of people as God worked Joseph's hard place to his good.

Ultimately God promoted Joseph to an amazing place—one where he was able to save two nations from starvation—Israel and Egypt.

And his relationship was restored with his brothers, who had betrayed him. "But as for you, ye thought evil against me; but God meant it unto good, to bring to pass, as it is this day, to save much people alive" (Genesis 50:20, KJV). Wow!

Joseph trusted God, and it worked mightily to his good. I surely wanted to be like Joseph. I wanted to lay my disappointments in life, my hurts, and all the broken pieces of my life at the feet of Jesus, just as he had. I wanted God to take my pain and my tears and turn it into glory—I wanted it all to have value and purpose.

I pondered it a lot—Joseph had to make a choice at some point. He was human, just like you and me, and I'll bet he was blindsided by all that happened to him. If I wanted to follow his example, I had to make that conscious choice as well, to trust God with it all, and to expect Him to work it to our good. Unfortunately, I've not always stayed on the right path, and I've definitely held my share of pity parties. I've whined and cried, but eventually, I've had to come up for air and recognize that I wasn't walking in faith or trust anymore. When I let the self-pity path enter, it birthed grief and bitterness, not joy and contentment.

When I recognized I was on that wrong path, just as I imagine Joseph must have done, I'd confess and get back on His path, the path of light, life, and hope. It was a deliberate choice—taking my eyes off myself and the hardships we faced and choosing to wallpaper my mind with His scriptures and believe what He said. And I'd read Joseph's words again: "As for you, you meant evil against me, but God meant it for good, to bring it about that many people should be kept alive, as they are today. So do not fear; I will provide for you and your little ones" (Genesis 50:20–21a, ESV), and I'd pray for God to use Jan's life and ours for His glory.

In the spring of 1988, God answered that prayer, but not exactly how I wanted it answered. Mike and I were invited to give our testimonies at the dedication Sunday of a new church. Dedication Sunday happened to fall on Easter Sunday—Resurrection Sunday. The only problem was that I'd made a vow many years before to never speak in public—but I'd do it this time since Mike was willing, and it seemed to be an answer to what I'd prayed.

I asked, "God, what do You want me to share?" I thought of the hours I'd spent studying scriptures on healing. It struck me what a miracle it'd be if God healed Jan on Resurrection Sunday. I imagined her withered little body uncurling as she stepped forth from her wheelchair. As I poured out my thoughts to the Lord, He spoke very clearly to my heart. "Pam, yes, it would be a wonderful miracle if I healed Jan on Easter Sunday, *but not nearly as great a miracle as one soul saved*!"

I had to let the truth of what He'd spoken sink in. I knew Jan would go into His presence when her life on earth ended and her body would be healed. But I realized that those souls who didn't know Christ had no such promise. Yes, one soul saved was truly a greater miracle than Jan stepping out of her wheelchair. My, how God was working in our lives.

The door that opened to give our testimony was the beginning of many doors that God would open to allow us to share about His grace. Since I didn't consider myself a speaker, it had never crossed my mind that God wanted me to share my testimony—verbally—out loud—on a stage—in front of people. *Surely not!*

Time Marches On

Another year rolled by, and Jan turned eleven on her birthday. Four months later, Ben turned sixteen. No one told me how traumatic it was to give your firstborn the car keys and watch him drive away for the first time. Having a driving teenager certainly kept me on my knees more than usual. All kidding aside, after we'd recovered from the shock of his first wreck, his being able to drive was a great blessing.

And time marched quickly by. January of 1990, we celebrated Jan's twelfth birthday. On her birthday, as I read my Bible, I was led to Isaiah chapter 42, the same Scripture God had given me when Jan was six months old. It again spoke to me, but this time I felt that God was calling me into a special ministry. I told my pastor that God had placed a call on my life. I didn't know what that call was, but I was so sure of His voice that I wrote in the front of my Bible:

> On Jan's twelfth birthday, God called me. Isaiah 42, which God gave me when Jan was a few months old, became clear—let me not turn back but be faithful.

Another Hard Place

The heart specialist had once predicted that Jan wouldn't live past twelve. He'd not mentioned that in several years, but Jan started out her twelfth year with an infection and terrible sleepless nights. After a week of antibiotics, the infection cleared up, but the sleepless nights persisted. Before I could find out what God had called me to do, it seemed all hell broke loose! (Which probably has more truth in it than I know since I'd felt God called me!)

Night after night after night, I was up with Jan until 3:00 and 4:00 a.m. Again, the nights were like wrestling with a colicky baby, except my "baby" now weighed nearly forty pounds. Through the terrible nights of earlier years, I was a young woman—now, at thirty-nine years old, it took its toll. I felt sorry for Jan, but I also wondered how long I'd be able to continue to care for her if the endless nights persisted. I prayed night after night, "Lord, please let Jan sleep tonight."

I stood on the scriptures about God giving His beloved sleep, always expecting that "tonight Jan will sleep." She didn't. I enlisted friends to pray. She still didn't sleep. People continually gave me advice on what to try next. What they didn't realize was that I'd tried everything. Jan was already taking more of her sedative than she should take, and given her heart problems, no other drug seemed to be available.

Lord, show me what to do? Jan and I are both desperate for sleep.

After eight weeks of little sleep, both Jan and I were exhausted beyond words. I again became a walking zombie, existing but not really living, once again watching my life go by. I still taught my Sunday school class, did my housework, cooked dinner every night, and went through the motions of living, but my joy was gone.

One morning my dear friend Ginger called. In my voice, she heard a discouragement that concerned her. *I thank You, Lord, for Christian friends.*

After our conversation, she prayed and asked, "Lord, what can I do to help Pam?" Immediately came the thought, *Take Pam the bag of tapes that are in the corner of your bedroom.* Ginger knew those thoughts were from God because she didn't remember that she had a bag of tapes in the corner of her bedroom.

In obedience, she looked. Yes, a bag that contained tapes lay under some papers. She remembered that her cousin had given them to her the summer before, and she'd forgotten all about them. She immediately got in her car and drove the fifteen minutes to my home.

The tapes were purely scriptures being read out loud with a background of soft, mellow music. One was entitled *Trust God* and contained only scriptures on trusting God; one was on *Fear Not* and contained the 365 scriptures on Fear Not. The other was In Christ and contained scriptures on *Who We Are in Christ*. As soon as Ginger left, I found my trusty Walkman, hooked it to my waist, plugged in the earphones, and listened to Trust God as I did my housework. I was certainly wallpapering my mind with His Word.

As I listened to the scriptures over and over, they cleansed my mind and pushed out the darkness that enveloped me by replacing those negative thoughts with His Word. My joy came back as my focus returned to His Word, not my feelings or my circumstances. For several days, I listened to the tapes constantly. My situation didn't change, but my attitude did, and my faith and joy returned. Only with God's help and His scripture could I continue on my path, and in His grace, God showed me that year after year after year!

One night as Jan began her usual routine of crying, I felt I had to have a few minutes of peace and quiet. Leaving her fussing, I crawled into bed and plugged in my scripture tape. I listened for a short time, and once again, the Scripture left me refreshed and ready to face another long night. As I removed the earphones, preparing to go back and calm Jan, I heard words forming in my mind. I quickly wrote down what I heard:

> My child, wherever you find your feet treading today, there is One who has walked there too. He left His home in glory and "pitched His tent" among us so that He might walk this path with you. He stands even now beside you, understanding your pain and suffering, having al-

ready nailed it to His cross. He says to you, my precious one, yes you, the one who suffers now, on that day I hung on the cross, My mind was on you. You see, I saw ahead to all the suffering through which you would tread, and I chose to go before you so that I could bear your burden today. Because of that battle I fought that day, I triumphed over sin. Now, precious one, grab hold of My words. They are life to those who find them and health to their bones. Grab hold, my child, open My Book, believe every word because I wrote them with My blood for you. Therein, if only you believe, you will find Me to be your strength, your joy, your deliverance, your shield, your peace, your health, your comfort, and much, much more. Grab hold...I will not forsake you if only you will believe.

Simplify, Pam

How faithful my Lord was, and what a gentleman! He never pushed me but always gently encouraged me to get back on the right path when exhaustion and discouragement threatened my walk. As always, His wisdom and His Word were my deliverance.

At this point, I'd done all I knew to do. Finally, I increased Jan's sedative dosage. She had evidently built up a tolerance to the old dosage. For the first time in a long while, she slept. I knew that not sleeping was slowly killing her, so I felt the increased sedative couldn't hurt her any worse. I told my doctor what I'd done, and he supported my decision.

Around this time, God also taught me another important life lesson. I was still attempting to do everything according to my self-imposed ideals—ideals formed prior to my caregiving days. I'd expected far too much of myself for a long time and just pushed harder to still do it all. Christmas dinner is a good example.

Mike's grandmother left me her 1899 Yale patterned china. I loved it. It was etched in gold around the borders and was beautiful. Her holiday tables were always set with it. I was blessed that she'd left it to me, and I set my holiday tables with it as well since I'd inherited it in 1979. It couldn't be put in the dishwasher, though, and had to be handled very carefully.

On Christmas Day, I found myself standing in the kitchen crying—still washing those dishes at 4:00 p.m.—long after the meal was completed and others had gone home. I'd been up almost all night. At 1:00 a.m. on Christmas Eve, I'd realized that Jan's frozen chicken trays were empty, and I stood deboning chicken at 2:00 a.m. I'd stuffed the twenty-pound turkey with homemade stuffing and put it into the oven at about 4:00 a.m. Jan cried and needed me at 5:00 a.m., and I never went to bed that night. At 4:00 p.m. on Christmas afternoon, as I washed those delicate dishes, I knew things must change. It had been an exhausting holiday for me, and I'd not enjoyed it.

As I prayed about it, God showed me that part of the exhaustion was self-imposed by me, myself, and I. I'd added one expectation of myself and then another over the years. That day I realized I was the only one that could take those self-imposed responsibilities off my shoulders. I determined then the next holiday would be different, and it was.

I bought Christmas paper plates, a nice turkey breast, and used Stove Top dressing for that next holiday. No one but me seemed to notice the major changes, but it helped this tired mama cope so much better. I also asked God to show me other areas where I could lighten my self-inflicted load.

God surprised me with the next thing He showed me. Jan was not a little girl any longer, but every night, I still changed her into pajamas around eight o'clock because that is what we do as moms! That was a difficult routine, given her body tightness and size. Her daytime clothes and her pj's were much the same—soft double knits with soft elastic at the waist. Unlike normal kids, she didn't walk around or crawl and get her clothes dirty. She wore bibs, and if she spit upon her clothes, I changed them immediately during the day. Yet, at eight o'clock at night, I changed her out of her clean knit clothes into a clean set of knit pajamas. That was clearly something I could change.

I also recognized that the whole chickens I bought weekly for Jan's food took a lot of my time to cook, debone, and freeze. I found a wholesale company where I could buy twenty to thirty pounds of boneless chicken breasts at a time, and they'd deliver them to our home. That saved me hours of time.

Yes, I learned a lot during this time that still carries over in my life today. I learned as mama's and caregivers, much of the time, we are the only ones who can make our own lives easier. If you are overwhelmed with your responsibilities, ask God what things aren't necessary.

After three nightmarish months, we began to get back to a new normal, and I focused once again on my call. I still didn't know what the call was, but I knew it was to help hurting people. The hurt and despair of the past three months were certainly very fresh on my heart. How many were walking in pain, too, without knowing the love and care of my Savior. How I longed to share with them.

Later in the spring, Mike, Jan, and I went to Tulsa for the weekend to visit our dear friends, the Yagers. On the trip back home, as I talked with Mike, I suddenly knew what I was supposed to do for the Lord. In fact, I said, "Mike, I can't explain it, but I know exactly what I am supposed to do for the Lord. I'm to write a booklet sharing the scriptures that have helped me to survive the past twelve years. I want to share them in a form that can fit in a purse easily, can be mailed easily, and can be placed beside someone's bed so that in a trial, at a glance, they can see the Word." I was so excited; I could hardly wait to get started.

That next day I began writing. I'd planned to share about Jan, but as I prayed, I felt the Lord encouraged me to be general about my sorrow, not specific. No one needed to know what my situation was. That way, whatever they were facing, they could apply the scripture in the booklet to their situation.

I knew I wanted the theme of the booklet to be following the Shepherd, but I had no idea how to get my typewritten pages converted into a booklet. God knew, though, and within a few weeks, everything came together.

The booklet started like this:

Dear Fellow Sheep,

If your heart is breaking, and the load you carry today seems unbearable, I write this, especially for you. I write it because I have walked there and still do. I pray that some of the answers I have found will also be answers for you.

When my painful journey began, I said, "I can't handle this. It hurts too much and is too hard!" The situation looked impossible, and I knew I didn't have the strength to carry on.

Then I began to hear, to really hear God's Word.

And the pages that followed primarily had the promises God had given me in the scriptures—scriptures that had been my life ropes in my storm.

As I thought of the many times my Shepherd had pulled me out of the darkness of despair by shedding the light of His Word into my heart, I knew I'd name my ministry Send the Light. That's what I wanted to do, send His Light to hurting people who needed Him.

By the summer's end, I'd printed three hundred *Follow the Shepherd for Comfort* booklets. Mike was very supportive—graciously paying all of the printing expenses. Of the original three hundred copies, I gave away many and sold enough of them to replenish my original cash outlay. This allowed me to fund my next printing. Each step of the way, I learned a bit more about binding, printing, etc. By my next publication, I was able to print one thousand booklets, and God began to lay other booklet ideas on my heart as well.

Mike and Ben helped me add color to the pages by using colored pencils. The booklet was about thirty pages long—each page was a bit bigger than an index card. I used our dining room table as a collating table, with thirty stacks with one hundred cards in each stack. We'd color little parts of certain pages—1, then 12, etc., and when they were colored, we'd walk around the table and collate each booklet. At first, I took them to an office supply company to be bound with a comb binder. Eventually, I bought a binding machine and bound them myself at home.

Nineteen ninety-one came, and with it came Desert Storm. Several *Follow the Shepherd for Comfort* booklets went to servicemen and their families. I was so blessed. Many called to tell me how the Word had ministered to them. One lady called and told me that her husband had died of cancer, and he'd asked her to read those *Follow the Shepherd* scriptures to him over and over for several days because they brought him comfort! I cried! Only God could do that.

Oh, Lord, only now am I beginning to see how mightily You have used a little girl named Jan who can't walk, talk, or use her hands!

Around this time, I was also asked to become a speaker for Christian Women's Club. The lady who contacted me asked me to please submit a tape of my testimony to their board. Since speaking wasn't part of my plan, I assumed it wasn't part of God's either! I didn't pray about it—I knew I wasn't a speaker, so I never made the tape. I was looking at my lack of ability, forgetting that God wasn't looking for my ability anyway; He was looking for my availability. He was my ability Provider.

God has an interesting way of steering us back on course when we veer in the wrong direction. One afternoon a friend dropped by for a visit, bringing with him an evangelist who had a healing ministry. They both prayed for Jan, and then the evangelist prayed for me. "The Lord impresses on my heart that He has called you to speak for Him. Don't turn down any opportunities that come your way to share for Him."

As I contemplated what he said, literally, the phone rang. Would you believe the caller was the lady from Christian Women's Club? "Pam, have you had a chance to make a testimony tape?"

"No, but I'll have it ready within two weeks!" I'd gotten His message!

By April, I had my first opportunity to speak for Christian Women's Club (I think it is now called the Women's Connection.) I enlisted several ladies to pray for me. I was scared! That day as I shakily stood to speak, the Holy Spirit strengthened me mightily. I could almost hear myself speaking as all fear left, and my testimony flowed forth.

What a joy to testify before a room of women that "God's grace does keep pace with whatever we face." And to think, if I had not stepped out of my comfort zone by an act of faith, I'd have missed such a blessing!

Christian Women's Club asked their speakers to always share this scripture toward the end of their testimony: "For I received from the Lord what I also passed on to you" (1 Corinthians 11:23a, NIV), and then I followed that with the plan of salvation. (Hereinafter, emphasis added.) I was amazed that in the twelve to fifteen years that I spoke for them, in over one hundred different places, many prayed that prayer of salvation—all because of a little girl who could not walk, talk, or use her hands. *Amazing!*

The Reason Behind My Reluctance to Public Speaking

It was my senior year in high school, and I was asked to give a pre-written speech at graduation. I don't remember why I was asked, but over fifty years later, I remember the first sentence of that speech.

It was: "My life is like a bright light shining," and at rehearsal, when I spoke my memorized lines, the speech teacher literally stood up and said, "*No, no, no*! You are flatting your 'eyes,'" at least that is what I thought she said! What she really said was, "You are flatting your 'I's'!" And she continued with, "You can't speak it that way."

I didn't know what "flat-ing my 'I's'" meant exactly, but I soon found out. I was given free speech lessons to learn "how not to flat my 'I's'!" and later, I understood that what I was saying was, "My lie'af is lie-ak a brie-ght lie-ght shie-ning!"

The speech teacher took me through exercises where she held my chin in her hand and told me precisely where to place my tongue so I would eliminate that "awful flatting 'I'" problem that she abhorred! Guess that's why I remember that line so well. I must have rehearsed that speech 5000 times to make certain I did not flat my "I's."

During my freshman year in college, I noticed that speech was one of the extra curriculum classes. And due to that "no, no, no" reaction in the free speech lessons in high school, I thought I must need that class!

The first time I stood to speak in my new college class, the teacher had a similar reaction to the high school teacher! I decided at that moment that once I got out of that class, I'd never stand before an audience again!

Fast forward twenty years, and I was asked to give my testimony for Christian Women's Club—and I quickly remembered my vow, and I'd declined. I didn't ask God; I just flatly said, "Thank you, but no." After all, I might flat my "I's"!

I would have missed so many blessings had I continued to focus on my lack of ability rather than on God's grace! It required that I take a huge step of faith—one outside of my comfort zone. Is there anything you need to rethink that God has asked you to do? He'll provide the ability and the strength. I can testify to that!

More Change

In the midst of all the changes of 1991, the month of May brought a very major one. Ben graduated from high school. It was a very emotional time for more reasons than one.

Knowing there would be several lengthy things that we'd want to attend with Ben, including graduation, we had to find care for Jan. It'd become harder to find babysitters for her, particularly ones who could lift her and feed her. Her previous teenage babysitters had grown up, and many of them had moved away.

We enrolled Jan for a two-week stay in the Cerebral Palsy Center. It's a center for handicapped children located in Norman, Oklahoma. It's about a forty-five-minute drive from our home. I'd visited the facility in early January and began the necessary steps to get Jan accepted for her two-week stay. In all of Jan's thirteen years, we'd never left her for more than three or four days. Those few times were always with someone that we knew well, and they came to our home. I'd never left her with strangers. I knew it would be a hard thing to do, but I really didn't realize how hard!

We arranged to take Jan to the Center the week before Ben's graduation. That gave us some special time alone with him prior to his actual "big event." Before I packed Jan's clothing, everything had to be labeled "Jan Whitley," even her socks. It made me think of a letter I'd received the week before from a sweet friend, Toni. In it, she told of the agony of having to place her son in an institution. Handicapped as severely as Jan, he grew too large for her to lift. Her letter described the pain of labeling his belongings the night before she took him to his new home.

As I stood doing the same thing, I thought of my friend and all the other mothers who'd at some point had to do what I was doing, only for them, it was permanent. I cried uncontrollably. I couldn't imagine how hard it was for them.

Morning came, and Mike and I reluctantly loaded Jan's things into the van. My heart was breaking. If you've never had a handicapped child, imagine taking a nine-or-ten-month-old child who isn't healthy and dropping them off with strangers. The CP Center was very understanding—they let us see which bed Jan would be in and where most of her time would be spent. They assured us that we could call and check on her anytime, twenty-four hours a day. But as we walked down the long corridor to the exit, we looked back and saw our innocent little girl sitting forlornly in the midst of many strangers. It took every ounce of strength we could muster to walk out and leave her. We both cried as we made the lonely drive back to our empty house.

I knew that the stay at the CP Center wouldn't be easy for any of us, but I was determined to have the extra time for Ben. He'd only graduate once from high school. I desperately wanted this time just for him.

Jan's health hadn't been good for the past three months. She'd had many sleepless nights and gradually dropped weight. At one point, she was down to thirty-five pounds. Her legs were beginning to look like toothpicks once again. We started giving her Ensure Plus twice a day in addition to her usual diet and finally got her weight back up to forty pounds. The Center would keep a close watch on her weight too.

Neither Mike nor I could sleep the first night Jan was gone. At about 3:00 a.m., I said, "Mike, isn't this crazy? We can't sleep with Jan here, and we can't sleep without her here!"

I called the CP Center. They said Jan hadn't been able to sleep, and they had rolled her bed off the ward to a private room across from the nurse's station. They had difficulty feeding her also.

Mike and I decided we'd better go see her the next day. So, the next morning after a night of little sleep, as soon as Ben left for school, we drove to the CP Center. I fed Jan so the staff could observe again how I did it, and we stayed for a couple of hours. Again, walking out and leaving her was as distressful as it had been the first time. *Lord, I never knew this would be so awful.*

We wound up going to the Center almost every day because Jan continued having difficulty eating and sleeping. She ran fever occasionally, and the night nurse said she had an episode of choking one evening that left her blue for a while. We were very concerned. We attended church Sunday morning prior to Ben's baccalaureate, and someone said, "Hey, this must be like a second honeymoon for you guys, not having Jan."

Mike and I just smiled, realizing, once again, that few understood our situation or knew the heartbreak we were enduring. The week went by and graduation day arrived. We attended the ceremony alone, saddened that there was no family to share his special day with us.

We realized that this would be our first and last child to graduate. It was bittersweet. The ceremony ended, and we walked out into the cool of the night, realizing that a new chapter in our lives was beginning. One that included Ben going off to college, but that was not all that was getting ready to happen!

God's Grace Keeping Pace

God was showing me clearly that He was using Jan's life and ours to minister to others from our hard place of struggle. I loved catching glimpses of His grace. There wasn't any situation that He couldn't work in—my job was to give it to Him and follow His lead via His scripture. Fear, anxiety, and negative feelings profited nothing. Let's keep looking for those glimpses of His grace.

Chapter 16
GOD WILL MAKE A WAY

"[…] I will make a pathway through the wilderness. I will create rivers in the dry wasteland" (Isaiah 43:19b, NLT).

June is normally the time that I plant my marigolds and work in the yard. It's a time that Jan enjoys sitting out back in her wheelchair, listening to the bird's chirp, tilting her face up to the Oklahoma wind.

In June of 1991, there would be no such days. We brought Jan home from her two-week CP Center stay and attempted to get back to normal. On Wednesday, June 12, Jan's fever climbed to 105.5°F in a short period of time.

I called Doctor Biehler. He said, "I think you'd better take her to the emergency room." We drove there quickly, expecting a short-term hospitalization.

We were placed on the newly redecorated children's wing of Baptist Hospital—the new modern decor gave it the "feel" of a nice hotel room—the "feel" being broken only by the traditional hospital bed and IV pole! That room would become our home for the next month as Jan literally fought for her life.

She was diagnosed with pneumonia, but her infection seemed

to respond well to the antibiotics. After two days in the hospital, it looked like we'd probably be going home by the weekend. Then the bottom seemed to drop out. Feeding Jan became next to impossible. She fought so during the feeding times that my body ached and hurt all over from the battle. At thirteen years of age, she was a little over a foot shorter than me and a strong little girl.

What could possibly be causing this reaction?

On the third night in the hospital, Jan stopped breathing for a few short periods. I called the nurse. She called the doctor, and he gave orders to place Jan on oxygen with a machine to monitor her saturation levels. The monitor's alarm went off time and time again all night long as Jan failed to take in as much oxygen as she should.

The next day the feeding problem became steadily worse. I was the only one who could feed her, and I was starting to wonder if I could physically last much longer. We'd not yet discovered that Jan had solid blisters covering the entire roof of her mouth, gum to gum. She had picked up a virus in addition to the pneumonia. The medicines in her food were burning the sores in her mouth each time I fed her. My poor baby!

By the fifth day in the hospital, weariness had consumed me once again, this time in a way I'd never experienced. It was not only physical exhaustion but emotional exhaustion as well. My heart ached as I saw Jan suffer. My body ached and hurt as if I had the flu from the physical battle with her. I felt I couldn't continue, yet I had no choice. I cried Saturday as I attempted to feed her. It took two other people helping me to hold her in order to get any of her food down.

On Saturday night, Jan slept very little. I spent the night sitting behind her in the hospital bed, attempting to keep her calm so that she wouldn't jerk out the IV. As the sun began to rise, she finally slept for a short time. A nurse helped me drag my tired body out from behind Jan. I stood shakily and slowly walked to the window and stared blankly out at the new day. I wondered what it would bring.

Since it was Sunday morning, I turned on the Christian radio station. One phrase in a song immediately caught my attention. *God will make a way when there seems to be no way.* Tears streamed down my cheeks. Once again, I felt my Heavenly Father's presence, and I knew He'd spoken to me. I didn't know how He was going to do it, but I'd trust that He would get us through this.

At this point, Mike had two clients whom he'd already scheduled major jobs for. Since he was Whitley Engineering and there were no other employees, he was trying to take care of those responsibilities and stay at the hospital as much as possible. It was a terribly stressful time. In the midst of it all, Ben hadn't chosen a college. He needed our direction terribly, but all I could do was spend time on the telephone with him. We talked late into the night many nights as I sat behind Jan in the hospital bed, my heart aching for both of my children.

On Sunday night, my dear friend, Carolyn, visited and decided to stay with me until Jan went to sleep. Jan never went to sleep! As the night progressed, Jan's breathing grew rapid and labored as she struggled to catch her breath. We, along with the nurses, tried everything we could think of to help her. I thought she would die before morning. I waited until 5:00 a.m. to call Mike, and at 6:00 a.m., Dr. Biehler arrived. He called in a pulmonary specialist.

For the first time since Jan was born, I realized that I couldn't push myself any further to take care of her. I'd reached my limit. I could barely stand or even think. Never had I felt so frightened and overwhelmed.

Lord, You promised You'd not forsake me, so please help us.

The specialist had a feeding tube placed down Jan's nose. That solved the feeding problem and also meant I wasn't the only one who could feed her. *Thank You, Lord!* He started her on a round of new medications. He scheduled the Respiratory Department to visit every two hours, twenty-four hours a day. Each time they ran a tube down her nose and deep suctioned directly into her lungs.

God further answered my prayer that morning by sending two precious friends from church to take my place so that I could go home. I went to bed and slept until 4:00 p.m. I went back to the hospital for a little while, but Mike wouldn't let me stay. He and my friend Ginger took the night. Jan didn't sleep but was better, even smiling and laughing for them—something she'd not done in days. Once again, we thought the worst was finally over—we were wrong!

Another good friend began staying most days with me since we were on such a roller coaster of never knowing what would happen. On Tuesday morning, the report was still good, and I relaxed just a little. Then on Tuesday afternoon, Jan's IV infiltrated her arm. It had to be moved elsewhere.

Her veins began to collapse, and I held her, sitting behind her for five hours as the nurses tried time and time again to replace the IV. If I could keep Jan sitting straight up in the bed, she could breathe better, and she didn't get as agitated. If I moved and arched her back, she'd slide down in the bed, and that jerked out the IV. This wasn't intentional on her part—just her reaction to fear of what was happening to her.

Finally, after five hours of seeing the needle go in a new place and infiltrate again, I was almost hysterical. Her blood was all down the leg of my pants from the many failed attempts. My dear friend, Brenda, took over for me so I could leave the room and regain my composure. When I came back, Jan had the IV in her foot—in a few minutes, it infiltrated. We were down to the "last foot." This one had to work, and thankfully it did.

Jan didn't pop back this time from the ordeal. By Thursday, our seventh day in the hospital, I realized our fight was getting harder by the hour. With a panicked expression on her face, Jan labored for each breath she took, using even her shoulders to draw in each precious breath. Now holding her in a sitting position was necessary for her to breathe. I wondered if I'd ever see her beautiful smile again.

At times, I found myself breathing with the rhythm that Jan breathed, subconsciously trying to help her grasp her much-needed oxygen. Because Jan loved music, I had her tape player beside the bed. Instead of playing her music (since, at this point, she was paying it no attention), I began to play mellow praise music interspersed with scripture tapes twenty-four hours a day. That changed the feel of the room because it placed the focus on God, not on what was transpiring. That was a tool of grace that God taught me to choose, and I'd use it many more times—in many other hospital rooms filled with heaviness.

A friend also sent me scripture cards that I'd made and sent to her the year before. I couldn't believe how much they ministered to our current situation. Someone taped them on the wall around the room. They were such a comfort.

"[…] My Presence will go with you, and I will give you rest" (Exodus 33:14, NIV).

"Have I not commanded you? Be strong and courageous. Do not

be afraid; do not be discouraged, for the Lord your God will be with you wherever you go" (Joshua 1:9, NIV).

"I can do all things [which He has called me to do] through Him who strengthens and empowers me [to fulfill His purpose—I am self-sufficient in Christ's sufficiency; I am ready for anything and equal to anything through Him who infuses me with inner strength and confident peace]" (Philippians 4:13, AMP).

"So we take comfort and are encouraged and confidently and boldly say, The Lord is my Helper; I will not be seized with alarm [I will not fear or dread or be terrified]. What can man do to me?" (Hebrews 13:6, AMP)

"Lord, when doubts fill my mind, when my heart is in turmoil, quiet me and give me renewed hope and cheer" (Psalm 94:19, TLB).

"He gives strength to the weary and increases the power of the weak" (Isaiah 40:29, NIV).

As daily I read those cards over and over, they strengthened me. Coming into Jan's room was like stepping onto Holy Ground. A couple of the therapists even commented, "I don't know what it is about this room, but I look forward to coming in here. I feel comfort and peace!" I knew they were feeling the presence of God.

On Thursday night, Mike and I both stayed with Jan. I'd always said that nothing ever took my desire to eat, but Mike and I both found ourselves unable to eat. We held each other and prayed together and once again laid our little girl on the altar. My mother's heart wanted God to take my suffering child so that she'd suffer no more. That wasn't His plan, though.

Friday came, and Jan's condition worsened. As I sat behind her, someone also had to sit at the foot of the bed to brace Jan's feet. She was struggling, so I physically could not handle her by myself. I'll never forget the sight of one of my precious friends sitting against Jan's feet, washing them with her tears, as my tears splashed on Jan's braided hair.

Later that day, I went home to rest for a short time. Alone in my empty home, I grieved for Jan. I grieved for the shattered dreams and for the normal little girl we'd lost in surgery thirteen years before. I grieved for the precious child that now lay dying. The tears never came, but rather from deep within, a wailing came forth that I'd never experienced before.

Oh, Lord, help me walk through this valley.

The outpouring of love that we received was unbelievable. Friends stayed with us—Jan's teachers and other staff stayed, and their love was like an ointment poured onto our weary hearts, helping us to walk through our "valley."

On Saturday, Jan seemed no better. On Sunday morning, at 4:00 a.m., the therapist came in to give Jan her next suction treatment. I crawled onto the couch in her room to sleep for a while. He finished, and I took my position again with Jan. Within forty-five minutes, she was struggling terribly to breathe. I watched the monitor as her oxygen saturation levels dropped lower and lower. I called the therapist back. This time as he suctioned, Jan coughed up a big chunk of phlegm. Her breathing went to normal. She drifted off into a peaceful sleep, no longer fighting for each breath!

The therapist and I were shocked.

I said to the therapist, "Bob, were you praying for Jan?"

"Yes, I've had her name on my refrigerator now for a week, and I've prayed for her every day." I learned that we were both praying when we had the amazing breakthrough.

After testing, the doctor's found that over a period of time, Jan had aspirated food into her lungs. That's what caused her pneumonia. She could no longer be fed orally. As soon as she was strong enough, she'd have a feeding tube placed.

Jan was in such a weakened state that it took another week for her strength to build up. One of my friends organized a schedule, and for the next two weeks, thirty "angels" came in pairs of two and took three-hour shifts, which started at 9:00 a.m. and continued to 9:00 p.m. This made it possible for me to sleep in the daytime—I rested enough that I could handle the nights. Thank You, Lord!

Without their help, I couldn't have handled the intensive care that still lay ahead. On July 1, after a week of convalescence, Jan was taken in for surgery to place a gastrostomy tube in her tummy. For the rest of her life, she'd be fed through that tube—no more ground chicken and pureed vegetables.

Jan made it through the surgery, and on July 5, we finally brought her home. We had "lived" at the hospital for a month. We were home, but Jan still required twenty-four hours a day care. She was connected to a feeding pump that fed her slowly twenty-four hours a day. I initially hated that. Maybe it was because, to me, it symbolized giving up one of the last of the normal things that Jan could do...eat.

I set up an "infirmary" in the den, and I slept on the couch in bits and pieces—getting up with Jan every hour. The totally liquid diet made her wet her diaper every hour all night, and she would cry. Again, we were dealing with a child who was like an infant but whose crying made her fever go up.

Even though she couldn't use her hands, when she cried, she cycled them across her tummy. When a gastrostomy tube is initially placed, it's a hose that extends about a foot from the tummy. (It's replaced with a "button," which is flush with the tummy after two or three months.) Until then, the hose had to be coiled up and taped down. If Jan accidentally got her hands tangled in it and pulled it out, it could be fatal. We absolutely couldn't let her cry. She had to be held most of every twenty-four hours.

Only three days after Jan came home from the hospital, I was scheduled to speak at one of the Christian Women's Club functions. It'd been scheduled long before Jan's illness. I didn't think that I had the strength, but I prayed and asked God what He wanted me to do.

He gave me a scripture that said, "Go and tell what mighty things the Lord has done" (paraphrased) (Mark 5:19, NIV). My dear friend, Diane Yakel, came to our home and kept Jan so I could go. I went, He gave me the strength, and several people accepted the Lord as their Savior that day. Thank You, Lord.

Slowly Jan returned to a "new normal," and by the fall, she was able to return to school. And, yes, Ben did make up his mind about which college to attend, and we sent him off to Oklahoma State University. It'd take me almost a year to regain my strength.

As difficult as that period of time was, it was a time of growing in faith. If we could survive the summer of 1991, we could survive about anything! And there would yet be many more trials!

God's Grace Keeping Pace

He was teaching clearly that praising Him pushed back my depression and self-pity. I needed to continue reminding my heart of His goodness when the seasons were tough and continue to praise Him. Let's keep looking for those glimpses of His grace—they are there.

Chapter 17
IN THE EYE OF THE STORM

"If you look at the world, you'll be distressed. If you look within, you'll be depressed. But if you look at Christ, you'll be at rest" (Corrie ten Boom).

Nineteen ninety-two dawned, and we celebrated Jan's fourteenth birthday. The gastrostomy tube proved to be a wonderful blessing, and I recognized that fact. Including the hours that it took each week to shop for Jan's food, prepare it, and then feed her—I now had an extra two to three hours a day. I couldn't believe it. It made life so much easier for me and eating so much easier for Jan. She didn't seem to miss eating at all either. Another plus was that her daddy could now feed her. It was interesting how I always fought change, and yet much of the time, it was a better place for us to be—where the change was!

Because Jan was now getting all of her nutrition and keeping it down, her weight went from forty-two pounds to sixty pounds in a matter of weeks. She suddenly "blossomed" into a teenager. Because she was on a totally liquid diet now, she also drooled profusely, and I made large bibs and had to keep one on her at all times. Those bibs helped to hide some of her little "blossoms." As she entered puberty, her daddy teased her. Going to the store, he brought her back a present—spray deodorant!

We still weren't without our sleep difficulties, and as Jan's weight climbed, I could no longer stand and sway her when she was fussy. Bad nights were really "bad" nights now, and my fatigue increased. If Jan was well enough to attend school and the temps were above seventy, I always picked her up because she still couldn't tolerate the heat.

The route I drove in our van took about twenty minutes. It involved a lonely and curvy not-heavily-traveled road, and I found myself fighting to stay awake. It scared me a time or two as I almost dozed off. I learned to grab a refrigerated pop as I left home, and rather than drink it, I'd hold it to my face—one side and then the other as I drove. That helped keep me awake. It was crazy but necessary at the time.

Spring came, and with it, an opportunity for me to go to a writer's conference. Once again, friends made it possible for me to go. After the conference, I knew that it was time to start writing Jan's story. I began in the spring of 1992 while sitting out back in the swing on my deck. Jan was there beside me in her wheelchair—and this year, we'd have our time to plant marigolds and enjoy the birds. I began to write:

> She sits quietly in her wheelchair, her head hung down and the drool coursing down her bib. She has a euphoric expression on her face as she drinks in each little sound of spring. She listens intently to those sounds—among them, the breeze rustling through the leaves. But most of all, she is delighted with the chirping of the birds. Our little dog runs by—his paws make a click-clack sound on the deck, and she giggles as if she thinks he'd made that sound just for her. She is so happy. She can't use

her limbs. She's never gotten her hands to her mouth. She can't speak, and the world labels her profoundly handicapped, but what simple things bring her joy and delight and what love she sheds forth into this world! The pure joy she has is something some search a lifetime for and never find. I wonder if, in heaven's eyes, she is really handicapped?

I also think writing about Jan helped me deal with the empty nest syndrome I experienced after Ben went to college. You have just finished reading a portion of what I wrote that spring day in 1992. Jan was then fifteen years old. I'm so glad I wrote what I did then because so many of the details would escape me now had I not written them down then.

On December 27, 1992, we took Jan to Children's Hospital to see the orthopedic specialist. She'd been very irritable for several weeks, and I'd observed a marked change in the tightness in her right leg. I thought perhaps she'd need another hamstring release.

After Jan was x-rayed, our doctor sat us down in another small room, looked us in the eyes, and said, "The good news is that it isn't Jan's hip or leg; the bad news is it's her spine."

He explained that in the fall of 1991, when we last had Jan x-rayed, the curve in her spine (brought on by the cerebral palsy) was at a fifty-degree angle. (Her curve is an "S" curve.) It had now progressed to an eighty-three-degree curve. Jan had more brain damage on the left side than the right, so her body pulled unevenly to the left.

"If it continues to progress, and I believe it will, it will lead to her demise. It will compromise her breathing as it compresses her organs. You could do surgery, but it is a major procedure, and given Jan's many problems, I can almost guarantee that she'd have serious complications." He then elaborated on the details of the surgery, and we knew we couldn't put Jan through such agony. What would she go through without it, though?

We drove home, feeling rather numb. It wasn't that we were afraid for Jan to die. It was that the suffering we had all endured in 1991 was too fresh in our memory. We couldn't bear to think of another episode like that, and Jan was twenty pounds heavier now. How could we manage?

It seemed that our lives were lived from one dire diagnosis to the next. That diagnosis, coupled with several other factors, plunged me into the deepest depression of my life. Certainly, the extreme fatigue was one major ingredient, and another was from having "relived" the past fifteen years in order to begin writing Jan's story. That had been very emotional, and so had Ben's leaving for college. With it all taken together, it was as if I had fallen into deep waters and I couldn't swim. I could see the glimmer of light at the surface of the water, but I couldn't reach it.

The enemy of my soul spoke loudly to my heart, and unfortunately, I listened. *"No one understands how you feel, Pam, because no one has walked in your shoes. What are you going to do? Jan is getting too heavy for you to lift."*

I didn't feel I could share my despair with Mike because he was a strong guy. He wouldn't understand my motherly heart that desired to care for my "baby" but was fast getting to the point that I couldn't. My body ached each time I picked Jan up, and that was when she wasn't hurting. What would I do if she was fighting due to pain? Again, fear spoke loudly to my mind with the *what-ifs* and *if-onlys*, and regrettably, I allowed all that anxiety to enter right into my heart. God never ever whispers with fear, guilt, despair, or worry. I should have recognized that old deceiver, but he got away with deceiving me with self-pity for a while.

In the midst of my despair, Jan continued to only sleep for two to three hours a night. When she'd awaken me with her crying at 2:00 or 3:00 a.m., I found myself crying also and praying repeatedly, *Help me, Jesus. Help me, Jesus.*

Since I could no longer physically sit and hold her for the rest of the night as I'd done for the previous fifteen years (she was just too big now), nor could I operate on two or three hours of sleep over an extended period of time, I realized I had to make a choice.

I put Jan in our spare bedroom on the other side of the house and walked away. I'd place a movie on the VCR for her to watch, and then I'd go back to bed. I knew that this was for her own good also because if I didn't get some rest, I couldn't continue to care for her. But I felt guilt for not being able to take care of her as well as I always had. (Again, guilt and fear are the enemy's tactics.) That thought process only added to my hopelessness.

Sometimes after I'd put Jan down to watch her movie, I'd pray the same prayer for another hour. *Help me, Jesus. Help me, Jesus.* After fifteen years, I no longer knew what to pray. I felt helpless. Laying back down in her room, I'd set a timer so that I could get up and check on her every hour till morning. This feeling of despair went on for about two weeks, with the events of each night further compounding them.

Mike was extremely busy at this time and under much pressure himself. I still kept the depth of my battle to myself—all bottled up where it continued to pressurize. But you know what, God sees it all and knows it all and cares like none other. He sends His comfort when we least expect it and in ways we can't imagine.

One day my friend Ginger and I went to lunch. I sat there, sharing very little but numbly listening as we ate our Mazzio's salad. And then what she said grabbed my attention, "Pam, I don't know what is wrong with me. I have never had a real bout with depression. I have no reason to be depressed, yet I feel this horrible despair. I can't explain it. It's a very hopeless feeling."

I was sitting there listening and thinking, *I can understand because that is exactly how I feel.*

Then she said, "Pam, this depression is so awful that I wake up in the middle of the night crying and saying, "Help me, Jesus! Help me, Jesus!"

When she said that, I stared at her in shock and disbelief. I didn't know how, but I realized it was not a coincidence that Ginger was describing my feelings. It took me a bit to gain my composure enough to speak, and then I blurted out, "Ginger, I don't understand what is happening here, but I think I know what is causing your depression. You have just described exactly what I am feeling. Not only are you somehow experiencing what I'm feeling, but you're praying what I'm praying. How can that be?"

We stared at each other in disbelief. After a moment of silence, Ginger said with a quivering voice, "Oh, Pam, I prayed that God would let me help carry your burden!"

After we'd dried our tears, we hugged each other, knowing that somehow, we'd been part of a miracle. We'd been prayer patterners for several years by this time, and we'd been through a lot together. She was my sourdough bread bringing friend when my dad was dying, and when her husband lost his arm in a car wreck, she'd called me, and I'd stayed with her children until her parents drove from Enid.

We'd been in Bible studies together, prayed together, and passed on books like The Hiding Place to each other. We'd been through pregnancies together. We'd often shared that we felt more like sisters than friends, but we'd never experienced anything like this.

Ginger then recalled that one night when Jan's seizures were terrible and I was hurting badly, she'd specifically prayed to help carry my burden. To our amazement, God had indeed answered her prayer and mine. He'd sent me help when I felt I was drowning. His grace truly does keep pace with whatever we face.

"Ginger," I said, "do you remember when your depression began?"

Looking back at her calendar, she surmised that her depression had begun about the time mine had, following my visit to the orthopedic surgeon. In His grace, He'd let her be a part of my despair, carrying my burden when it was too heavy for me to bear alone. And to think, I'd thought no one could know how I felt.

I knew if *God* would do something that precious for me, that even the part of the journey that yet loomed ahead, I'd be able to handle with His grace.

Later I asked Ginger if that was the end of her despair, and for the most part, it was. She learned that if that feeling began to come upon her, she needed to pray for me. Thank You, Lord!

That revelation of God's love and care for me, coupled with an essay that Ben wrote for a college class, were the two life ropes that God extended to me to pull me out of my depth of despair.

In Ben's essay, one of his wise paragraphs said,

If people just realized that having a handicapped child is not just something that happens to a child, it is something that happens to an entire family. It is something that makes their life totally different from everyone else's. If only they knew. My mom is not a normal mother with a handicapped child; she is a handicapped mother with a handicapped way of life. Her daughter's life is her life. She sleeps when her daughter sleeps. She hurts when her daughter hurts, and in the same way, when her daughter dies, a special part of her life will die too.

That essay put into words what I couldn't voice myself, and it ministered to my heart in a special way. Only God had known what I needed, and He provided it so magnificently. Once again, I could walk in His peace and His joy even in the midst of my raging storm.

As if to give me one more encouraging word, God allowed me yet another special blessing as He pulled me out of my pit of despair.

On the same day that I was writing about the neurologist who said Jan should be put into an institution, my friend Judith called. She didn't know that I was writing about "Dr. X."

She said, "Pam, do you remember 'Dr. X'?"

"Yes, I sure do!"

"Well," she continued, "I know his former wife. They divorced a while back. She has cancer and has been battling for her life. I sent her a copy of your Follow the Shepherd for Comfort booklet. I saw her last week, and she walked over and gave me the biggest hug. She said that while she was going through chemotherapy, she kept that little booklet in her purse and read it each day as she took her chemo. Pam, she told me that the scripture in that booklet literally gave her the strength to go through her ordeal."

I had to think about that for a moment. Without Jan, Follow the Shepherd for Comfort wouldn't have been written. I was amazed. God had used a little girl who could not walk, talk, or use her hands to reach a loved one of the very doctor who, in essence, said Jan's life was of no value. What a mighty God we serve. What a caring Shepherd.

And with that spine development that we could do nothing about, we once again asked a group of people to gather at our church altar and lay hands on Jan and pray. It was a precious evening as we surrounded Jan, anointed her with oil, and poured our hearts out to God on her behalf. I took pictures of Jan's back before we went because I knew God could visibly straighten her spine, and I wanted to have pictures to prove it. Afterwards, her spine looked no different as far as I could tell, but Jan's pain seemed to stop. Thank You, precious Lord.

God Grace Keeping Pace

He was teaching me that even a whisper such as, "Help me, Jesus," was heard by Him. We, as His sheep, weren't made to carry our burdens alone either. I had to keep looking for His multiple glimpses of grace.

Chapter 18
COUNT YOUR BLESSINGS

"My brethren, count it all joy when you fall into various trials, knowing that the testing of your faith produces patience" (James 1:2–3, NKJV).

1993

When I first began writing Jan's story, these were my circumstances; I had a daughter who was fifteen years old and could not walk, talk, or use her hands. She weighed sixty-two pounds, and I changed her and bathed her as if she was a baby. If I am honest, I really didn't want to walk where I was walking. I was exhausted! I didn't want Jan to have to walk there either because I saw her suffer in her twisted little body, but that is where we lived. During that season, there were many stories in the Bible that impacted me greatly: they gave me strength and perspective.

Remember, Joseph was betrayed by his brothers, who hated him and sold him into slavery. Then while he was a servant, he was falsely accused of rape and locked in prison. Through it all, what a great example Joseph was as he trusted God's hand, no matter what happened. He never pitied himself nor blamed God or others, and his obedient heart benefited thousands upon thousands of people, including the very ones who sold him into slavery. What an example! I wanted to learn to walk like him—filled with a heart of trust in God no matter what occurred in my life. That is where contentment and joy live.

Then there was the story of David and Goliath found in 1 Samuel. David applied God's truths too. He went up against Goliath with a slingshot and a few rocks and killed that mighty blaspheming giant. I wanted to have that God-kind of faith.

I could go on and on about Bible truths that impacted me, but I'll just share one more. In the book of Exodus, Moses and the children of Israel were in a seemingly hopeless situation. They were trapped against the Red Sea with no way of escape from Pharoah's massive army. As Pharoah raced toward them, Moses believed God above his dire circumstances: "Moses answered the people, 'Do not be afraid. Stand firm and you will see the deliverance the Lord will bring you today. The Egyptians you see today you will never see again'" (Exodus 14:13, NIV). Moses, by faith, stepped into that raging sea—onto dry land as he trusted and expected God's deliverance. God was faithful— He kept that ground dry, and the sea congealed until Moses led the children of Israel safely to the other side, and then God collapsed the water upon Pharoah and his army as they sought to follow and destroy God's people…God destroyed them instead.

It was clear to me that all those victorious Christ-followers I'd read about triumphed over their hard circumstances because they… believed…God. They didn't allow self-pity, fear, blame, or unforgiveness to set up residence in their hearts. Their God-given victory came in response to them believing God's written word and taking every thought captive that didn't line up with what God said. I knew I could do that too because God had/has not changed. When He said to take every thought captive in Corinthians, that is what He meant. His Word and His Holy Spirit were mighty to help me, but it was me that had to know what He said and then apply His word to my circumstances. "We destroy every proud obstacle that keeps people from knowing God. We capture their rebellious thoughts and teach them to obey Christ" (2 Corinthians 10:5, NLT).

In the earlier chapters of this book, I shared how The Institutes drilled into us that we must fill Jan's brain with the input it lacked by bombarding her senses with frequency, intensity, and duration. Without realizing it, this was a principle that I needed to apply to myself—inputting His words, His thoughts, and His directions in any way I could to strengthen myself and override my negative thoughts. In essence, I was renewing my mind just as God had instructed me to do in Romans 12:2a (NIV): "Do not conform any longer to the pattern of this world, but be transformed by the renewing of your mind."

This kept my focus where it needed to be—interpreting my life through the lens of His truth, and it kept my eyes off the long dark nights yet looming ahead. It pulled me toward His peace. I'm not saying I did this perfectly, but I am saying these chosen paths/inputs would always get me back on His path—the path of contentment and joy.

Over the years, I also collected tools to navigate my difficult seasons. These tools equipped me with strength, renewed my hope, and renewed my peace, even when the nights were long and the circumstances didn't change. I'll share my favorite seven:

1. *Scripture and Prayers.* There were many seasons I didn't feel like reading my Bible or praying because I was exhausted and living in survival mode. But when I spent time with God and prayed, His written Word brought me His strength, comfort, and hope. When I was too fatigued to concentrate, I found it very helpful to journal the

scriptures I read, write down what I felt He was speaking to me, and journal my prayers as well.

I also had a couple of small books that were the promises of God—again, promises that gave hope, promises for strength, promises for peace, etc. ...they were categorized and helped me focus my thoughts.

During this time, I also memorized James chapter 1...here's a snippet...

> Consider it pure joy, my brothers and sisters, whenever you face trials of many kinds, because you know that the testing of your faith produces perseverance. Let perseverance finish its work so that you may be mature and complete, not lacking anything. If any of you lacks wisdom, you should ask God, who gives generously to all without finding fault, and it will be given to you.
>
> James 1:2–5 (NIV)

So many great devotionals, podcasts, and Bible studies are available today too. My son has limited time, but he pours in truth from podcasts as he drives to work. I love that.

Find a way that works for you. If you are grieving, GriefShare has its own daily devotional geared for grievers. You can subscribe to it, and I did when my grief was fresh. If you are reeling from a divorce, I believe DivorceCare also has devotionals online too.

2. *Choose to Listen to Uplifting Music.* Music was one of my biggest comforts and still is. It could play in the background no matter what I was doing, and I learned to always pack my CD player when we were in the hospital. Of course, at home, Jan's music filled our house

for years. I remember often singing along with her songs. In fact, our whole family sang along. She loved the Psalty, the singing songbook series. Those CDs filled our home with joy—songs like "I've Got the Joy, Joy, Joy Down in My Heart" and "This Little Light of Mine," and one of my favorites, "Have Patience." Those songs were lifesavers in more ways than one. They put joy in my heart right now as I write this, just recalling them.

Today, with YouTube, earbuds, and iPhone, it's easy to keep amazing music flowing constantly. That's why I chose to name each chapter in this book by a song title. The titles bear the name of a song that helped me cope and walk in peace.

3. *Choose Blessing Counting.* On my worst days, I was tempted to give in to self-pity. Somedays, I'd start down that self-pity road, but then I'd recognize those good-for-nothing thoughts, and I'd change my focus and count my blessings instead. Sometimes the blessings I counted were as simple as giving thanks for a handicapped parking spot close at hand. Sometimes they were as broad as giving thanks for all my appliances, my air-conditioned car, or my cool house on a summer day.

And sometimes, it was very random things that changed my focus. When we moved back from Texas, our new house had a secret green belt at the end of our cul-de-sac. There was a concrete sidewalk that led to it. Ben and our neighborhood kids played there a lot, and I'd walk down often to check on them. I learned that the area was dug out by settlers in the land run, and they'd spent their first freezing-cold Oklahoma winter hunkered down in that red clay dugout.   On a particularly hard day, I'd think about those courageous people. Many of them are buried on a hill above that dugout area in a sweet history-filled cemetery. What hardships they must have faced as they made their way to Oklahoma, many probably aboard rickety-old wagons. Just the thought of their situation humbled me and turned my eyes toward my many modern conveniences and multiple blessings.

I still use my counting blessings practice today. During the isolated COVID-19 days of 2020 and 2021, my hubby and I delighted in the many birds and critters that visited our yard daily. We've kept a log of the varieties we've seen, and we've written down well over fifty types of birds. We've photographed them and learned a lot about them. I enjoy sharing their pictures on Facebook, particularly for those people who are isolated and possibly alone.

Counting blessings doesn't change my circumstances, but it does change my focus and my attitude, and it brings me joy and strength as well because it takes my focus off what is not lovely, true, and good in my life and my world.

Lord, give us eyes to see the multitude of blessings that surround us each day.

4. *Choose Godly Friends.* When I first moved to Yukon, I was a fairly new mom, still homesick, and very lonely. We were searching for a new church home, but I'd not connected with anyone yet. A neighbor knocked on my door and asked if I'd be willing to host a Tupperware party. I quickly said yes and passed out invitations to my entire neighborhood the next week.

At that party, I met a young woman named Ginger. She was new to the neighborhood, too, and lonely as well. We became fast friends. She is still a dear friend forty-seven years later.

We both loved our families, loved God, and desired to be good moms. She taught me to make sourdough bread, and I taught her to sew knit T-shirts. We grew together in skills and in the Lord as we took

Bible studies together and shared play dates with our two children.

Mike and I also made finding our new church home a top priority as well, and we soon found more like-minded new friends to do life with. We did this in the beginning when we first married, and then in each move, we've made throughout our lives.

My precious friends have been invaluable to me in my seventy-year journey. They have refreshed my soul, inspired and encouraged me in my race, and come along beside me when life was too hard to walk on my own. "[…] a sweet friendship refreshes the soul" (Proverbs 27:9b, MSG). And I love this quote by author Jim Rohn too: "You are the average of the five people you spend the most time with." Choose friends wisely. Choose those who refresh your soul as you, in turn, refresh theirs.

5. *Choose to Focus Outward.* Often, when Jan was sick, she and I would be homebound for weeks. At times, I'd find myself entertaining poor-me thoughts as I gazed day after day at the written schedule of medicines, feedings, and suctions that hung on my refrigerator door, often with my timer set to remember them all, as the thought of the long night lay ahead. My circumstances were hard, but self-pity profited no one, least of all me. When I recognized I was in poor-me mode (inwardly focused), I learned to choose a direction change and look outwardly for others who were hurting.

Sometimes, I'd bake cookies for a neighbor who was going through a rough patch, or I'd send a card, or I'd call someone that God brought to mind. And even today, when I recognize that my heart is entertaining old-age thoughts of self-pity or I'm missing my loved ones who are no longer here, I gently remind myself to look for opportunities to bless others.

My daughter-in-love, Stephanie, does this focus-on-others better than anyone I know. My husband, John, wasn't feeling well heart-wise last year and was cooped up a lot. On one of those hard days, a puzzle arrived at our front porch from Amazon, sent by her. He went right to work, putting it together. John and I love to RV, and, on another day, a little Lego RV arrived. Again, he smiled and put it together. I'm looking at it right now—he has it displayed. It brought him joy, mainly because her kind act touched his heart.

Angie, my sweet stepdaughter, is also great at this. She has often had puzzles made from our pictures that we take on our travels and then surprised us with not only a puzzle project to enjoy but a beautiful memory to savor. These girls surely know how to bless us and others in dark days.

Today, we live in a world filled with needs. Sadly, I don't focus outwardly enough, but I am still blessed when I do pause and ask the Lord to show me who needs encouragement. Then I can text a note, write a card, or pick up the phone and call them.

Many scriptures encourage us in this manner. "Carry each other's burdens, and in this way you will fulfill the law of Christ" (Galatians 6:2, NIV). "Share with the Lord's people who are in need" (Romans 12:13a, NIV). "[…] whoever refreshes others will be refreshed" (Proverbs 11:25b, NIV).

Lord, help us to choose to be heart touchers and refreshers.

6. *Consider Reading Christian Books.* Reading what others overcame has always encouraged my heart, taught me the hows, and given me courage to keep walking. Corrie ten Boom's *The Hiding Place* was life-changing for me. Then, I read Joni Eareckson's book Joni, and later I devoured Catherine Marshall's books *A Man Called Peter* and

Beyond Ourselves.

One of my favorite books still is *Calm My Anxious Heart* by Linda Dillow. And at another point in my life, Barbara Johnson's books blessed me so much that I couldn't wait for her next one to be published…she has an amazing story.

She lost two of her sons exactly five years apart, one in Vietnam and the other in a car wreck, and her husband was stricken with brain damage. She entered into a very deep depression…but along the way, she learned to change her focus and view her pain through God's Word. When she did that, she went from a deep depression to a woman who was a powerhouse for God. I loved her lesson-filled books. I often read them while I held Jan. Most times, I had to read them in snippets—bits and pieces here and there—as I rocked Jan late into the night. Time and time again, other saints' experiences would bless me, giving me comfort and determination as they better equipped me for my battle.

Today, there are so many helps available. I listen to sermons, Bible teachers, and books via my phone. I can do it as I put on my makeup or when I soak my body in Epsom salts. My friend, Sue, has inspired me to multitask. She listens to uplifting messages while she is cooking, ironing, walking, and driving.

7. *Seek Out Faith-Filled Mentors*. The definition of "mentor" is an experienced and trusty advisor. I believe the God-kind of mentors encourage us to trust God as we see their beautiful example of how to love and serve God, no matter what we are going through.

One of my favorite mentoring examples from the Bible is Mary, the mother of Jesus, tenderly mentored by Elizabeth, the mother of John the Baptist. Naomi and Ruth's relationship is another example that blesses me.

I've been richly blessed with wonderful mentors. When I married at nineteen, one of my first mentors was Mike's boss's wife, Liz. She taught me many things about homemaking and about being a good wife and mother. Phyllis Poe and her husband, Jack, our pastor, were wonderful mentors as well. They walked beside us through the early days of learning to cope with Jan's brain damage. Gay Wilkerson, who gave me Psalm 139 in the chapel at Children's, was another wonderful mentor and dear friend. She has been beside me throughout most of my hards—encouraging me and feeding me scripture, and she's come along beside me to help when needed. Each of these mentors taught me different aspects of how to walk in light of God's word. Some of them have been lifelong mentors, others have been for brief seasons, but it seemed when I felt alone in my struggles, God sent me encouragement and help via them.

If you don't have a mentor, ask God for one. Sometimes, it may take a bit of time, but He'll send the one you need. Look expectantly for His provision.

A Well-Lived Life That Mentored Me

One such prayer was answered in my forties when I was exhausted and struggling. In spite of my pain, I was teaching a Bible study for older women at our church. It was a rather selfish sacrifice of time because those ladies always blessed me, and the preparation did too. A new lady named Ruth Buchanan joined our group. Each time she shared, I listened intently because of her wisdom. Peace and joy radiated from this eighty-plus-year-old saint each time she shared. She practically glowed. I really wanted to know her story, and I asked if I could schedule a visit with her soon.

A few days later, I entered her tiny apartment and once again hung on each word she shared, "Honey, I have been through quite a few hard places, and I can testify that the Lord has never failed me—not even once." I learned as she talked that she was also a writer, and she showed me several spiral-bound notebooks yellowed with age and filled with her story.

She wrote much of what follows: "On a hill in Texas stand five little crosses, four mark the graves of four of my six children, and one marks the grave of my husband."

Because of Jan, she began her story by telling of her own experience with her handicapped child, a precious little girl who lived to be only two. That little girl died in her arms at only two years of age. Her eyes watered as she talked of the heartbreak of that day.

Then she told of the full-term baby who died when her placenta ruptured. She was home alone, and she came close to death herself. Her life blood was almost drained from her body when her husband found her passed out on the floor and rushed her to the hospital. (We're probably talking about the 1950s.)

Then she shared of a vacation trip where one of her sons was bounced headfirst onto a concrete sidewalk from a hammock as he played with several children. He suffered brain damage and only lived a few days. By then, I was crying.

"With three of my precious children already buried on that hill, I thought I was clinging to God as close as anyone could. But I was wrong because that was before!"

The rest of her story poured forth. In their fifties, her husband went heavily into debt as he turned their farm into a working dairy. She said to him one day, "Honey, if something happened to you, what in the world would I do?"

He responded, "Sweetie, don't you worry, if something happened to me, Charles [their thirty-year-old married son] would know how to handle everything."

A few weeks after that discussion, her husband and that thirty-year-old son were both killed in a small plane crash.

"I went into shock," she shared as the pain of that day was still written on her face. "And there were still all those cattle that had to be milked that night."

She said neighbors and church friends kept the dairy up and running through the funerals…then the reality of her situation hit her hard. She had no education, no money, much debt, a dairy farm to run, and two children to still raise.

She'd write her daily needs on paper and shut herself into the bathroom (because that was where she could be alone with God) as she cried out to Him, "God, either You are who You say You are, or You are not! Here are my needs, and You know I have absolutely no way to meet them."

She radiated His grace as she said, "Over and over and over again, He'd meet them."

As she continued her story, I learned that in the years that followed, Ruth sent her two remaining children to college and fought and won a battle with breast cancer.

She said, "God proved to me that He is exactly who He says He is! Would you believe, He even made a way for me to go to the Holy Land because I told Him that was a desire of my heart!"

I was amazed by her story and so blessed. Then she prayed for me and asked God to provide for me as He had for her. She also prayed that God would make a way for me to have help with Jan. God answered her prayer before too many months had passed.

I have been blessed by several other mentors through the years, and their input has been invaluable. I thank God for each of them. Remember to pray and ask God for special mentors in your life.

Here's the recap of the above tools I shared: "Seven Tips" to help with your hards in life.

1. Let's attempt to read the Bible and to pray.
2. Let's attempt to listen to uplifting songs.
3. Let's attempt to count our blessings.
4. Let's attempt to choose godly friends.
5. Let's attempt to focus outwardly.
6. Let's attempt to read books by Christian authors that have triumphed.
7. Let's attempt to seek out victorious mentors.

Chances are, if you are walking in a hard place today, you may already be putting most of the above tips into operation, but if you aren't, I encourage you to do so. It will help you.

And let's be aware of what we are speaking into our circumstances each day as well—let's make certain our words align with what God says. For example, if we are saying, "I can't handle this," or "This is too hard," that isn't what God says to us. Let's refocus our thoughts and speech to align with His Words. "I can do all things through Christ who strengthens me" (Philippians 4:13, NKJV).

Another example would be saying, "If something bad can happen, it happens to me." Or "Nothing ever works out for me," or "Nothing good ever happens to me." Let's align our words with what God says. "So do not fear, for I am with you; do not be dismayed, for I am your God. I will strengthen you and help you; I will uphold you with my righteous right hand" (Isaiah 41:10, NIV). "This is the day the Lord has made. We will rejoice and be glad in it" (Psalm 118:24, NLT). This may seem silly to some, but to change our focus, we also have to change our outlooks and our expectations.

My prayer for you right now is that God will make a way for you to walk in victory, that He will send mentors to pour into your life, that He will put an uplifting song in your heart, and that He will speak a scripture of hope to your heart as well. May He be your strength, joy, and your Mighty Refuge no matter what hard place you are walking.

God Grace Keeping Pace

God's grace is always tucked in the hards we face. He'll send us books at unexpected times in unexpected ways. He'll send us mentors in unexpected places, He'll send scriptures at the perfect time, and songs will float through the airways when we need them the most. Let's always look for glimpses of His grace.

Chapter 19
JESUS LOVES ME

"Thy words were found, and I did eat them; and thy word was unto me the joy and rejoicing of mine heart" (Jeremiah 15:16a, KJV).

The summer of 1994 was difficult, and I struggled to walk in joy and contentment—the place I most wanted to learn to walk. Jan slept very little, and her weight nudged eighty pounds. One day God blessed me with the following nugget as I was about to fall into self-pity once again:

As I washed dishes at the kitchen sink, the spirit of heaviness clung to me like a wet blanket, weighing me down. In the middle of my pity party, I heard Jan choking.

I hurriedly dried my hands and rushed to her side. She lay on the floor in front of the console television, watching her favorite movie, *Little Mermaid*. I sat her up and, with my hand cupped, rapped her on the back several times until she caught her breath. I wiped the drool from her mouth, hugged her, and let her return to enjoying the ocean and fish sounds that she so adored in that movie.

This was a typical day for the two of us when Jan wasn't at school—me listening for any sounds of distress and Jan enjoying life between seizures and strangling coughs.

Though Jan still functioned at the level of a two-to-six-month-old infant, one of the blessings of that was her innocence. She didn't anticipate bad things or worry about anything. I, on the other hand, could easily hop on a track of worry if I didn't fight it hard. *Would Jan have a seizure and bite through her lip? Would she choke one day and not be able to catch her breath, or would I find that she'd passed away one morning when I entered her room?*

Back at my dishwashing post, the anxiety of all those what-ifs engulfed me. It's been said that worry doesn't empty tomorrow of its sorrow, but it empties today of its strength. That is the truth. As I was about to allow myself to be emptied of my strength, I talked to God instead.

God, You seem so distant. Do You really care about me? Do You really love me? Do You really love Jan?

As quickly as those thoughts of despair came, they were replaced with,

Pam, do you love Jan?

Of course, I love her with all my heart.

Why do you love her?

Because she is my daughter.

And that's the same reason I love you. You're my precious daughter.

Suddenly the despair and heaviness lifted. Jan and I were both His, and He loved us with His everlasting love. He never slumbered or slept, and I wasn't walking this way by chance but by design—His design. He had a good plan for both of us, and He has a good plan for you as well.

A few months later, I was invited to do an interview with a local pastor for his weekly television show. He'd heard about Jan and asked me to share my testimony. After the recording was finished, the pastor's wife approached me and said, "Hello, I'm Rod's wife. Thank you for sharing your story." Then she looked searchingly into my eyes and said, "May I ask how you are really doing? You look so exhausted."

My normal response was always the standard, "I'm fine," but her caring look touched my heart deeply, and I responded honestly, "I am exhausted."

With concern in her voice, she said, "My daughter is doing her nursing internship at the Children's Center in Bethany, Oklahoma. It's one of only seven critical-care pediatric nursing centers in the United States. They do an incredible job. Would you promise me that you'll give them a call? I think you need their help!"

Before I knew it, I said yes!

Back at home, I was mad at myself because I'd promised her to call that center! I looked up the mileage, and it was only five miles from our front door, but I really didn't want to call them. My heart's desire was to take care of Jan as long as she lived, and I can honestly say I assumed because that was my heart's desire, it was God's too. Unfortunately, I hadn't asked Him. But the next day, because of my promise, I looked up their telephone number and called. The receptionist answered and said, "Let me have you talk to one of our social workers."

The social worker was very kind but told me they didn't provide any temporary care. Then she asked, "Is your child a total care child?"

"Well, I don't know if she is or not."

"Would you mind telling me a little about her?"

"She is a delightful little girl! She laughs and giggles and loves to listen to music every waking hour."

"Can she walk or talk?" she asked with tenderness in her voice.

"No."

"Can she feed herself?"

"No," I replied. "Her cerebral palsy is so severe that she has never had any purposeful movement of her hands, and she is fed through a gastrostomy tube and wears diapers."

There was a moment of silence, and then the social worker said softly, "Honey, she is a total care child."

I was so close to Jan's care that I didn't even know she'd be considered a total care child!

And then she said, "Would you promise to take a tour of our facility? I think you'd love it!" And before I knew it, I had made another promise.

I don't remember when I actually called to take that unwanted tour, but it was sometime after the decision was made by the Federal Government that all handicapped kids had to be sent to school with their peers.

That took Jan out of her little neighborhood school program that she'd attended since she was three. It was a wonderful program, staffed by people who'd known our sixteen-year-old Jan for thirteen years of her life. The sweet nurse had been Jan's nurse since Jan was three as well and was wonderful with her. This program was in an older neighborhood. When the community aged, and there were fewer elementary-aged kids in that district, the administration wisely took a whole wing of the school and redesigned it specifically for handicapped kids. It crossed district lines and was a hub of well-thought-out provision for handicapped kids from a large radius of Putnam City schools.

They allowed the remaining non-handicapped elementary wing choices in their curriculum; one choice was to work an hour with our handicapped kids, and many wanted to. It was a great program, and that sweet school became an extended family for many parents and helped us to walk in our difficult shoes.

This new Federal Mandate would send Jan and her schoolmates to a regular high school. I fought it all the way to the Oklahoma's State Capitol, and for a while, the attorney general thought we were going to win the fight, but we lost.

I visited the high school program and was very disappointed in it. Those high school kids were Jan's age, and that part was true, but they were not her peers. To make matters worse, I returned home that day and received a call from the high school asking if Jan would like to try out for the Pom-Pom squad. I cried, and I felt anger over the loss of our safe-haven school. I knew I couldn't send Jan there, and without school, Jan's chair was so awkward; I wouldn't be able to buy groceries because I couldn't push a grocery cart and her chair. What would we do?

So, on a hot summer day, I toured the Children's Center. I walked through the scripture-lined hallways of their bright, cheerful old building, and I saw how wonderfully cared for the children were. I was so aware of God's presence that I cried, and I knew then I'd just toured Jan's new home.

After visiting with the Children's Center's social worker, Barbara, I learned that to be accepted as a resident, we'd have to apply to a team called OBRA. Their team was comprised of a nurse, a social worker, and a psychologist. They'd visit our home and determine if we needed the services the Children's Center offered.

Those services weren't covered by insurance, so OBRA would make the decision on the Children's Center taking Jan. I was told that seldom would OBRA vote for placement because their goal was to always keep the child at home. After Mike and I prayed about it, we decided that if this was God's next step for us, OBRA would have to vote "yes" on Jan with their first visit.

Over the next week, they scheduled their home study, and I did all the things we needed to do if Jan was going to be accepted at the Children's Center.

On the meeting date, when the team visited our home, they were extremely thorough and very professional. They asked a lot of questions and took many notes. I had no idea what they felt about the visit. But within the next couple of weeks, I received a call from the Children's Center, and OBRA had voted unanimously that Jan needed the care the Children's Center provided. Once again, I cried!

Within days of that call, events lined up for Jan to enter there as a resident. It was not a door I'd ever expected to walk through!

You see, I'd always really believed I'd take care of Jan at home as long as she lived—so preparing for this placement hadn't been something I saw coming. It was a terribly hard and unexpected grief to face.

Each night, I sat in our old leather chair and rocked Jan, realizing that soon these precious times would end. My tears kept Jan's long braided hair damp as I prepared my heart for her departure.

The realization that Jan would never live at home again was horrific for me. I sat on the floor of her room with her beside me with a Sharpe in hand as I labeled all of her clothes. It seemed Jan had a thousand socks and hair bows…I cried as I labeled each. She had many music CDs—which I labeled too. Going through her things and labeling them was one of the most painful things I'd ever done….it forced me to imagine Jan in a setting that was not home with us but with strangers.

Three weeks filled with endless heartbreak passed, and the placement day dawned. We'd partially packed the van the night before, and I finished loading it that morning.

"Help me, Lord," I cried as the tears poured. I rolled Jan to the van, loaded her, and started our five-mile drive! Mike was still self-employed, and the date fell on a day that he was in the middle of drilling a well. I was rather glad that he wouldn't have to face the painful logistics of that day, and thankfully, God provided mightily for me.

Arriving at the facility, I pulled into a handicapped parking space. With my heart heavier than her wheelchair, I let the lift down, and Jan and I rolled toward the center's entrance. The head of the Children's Center stood in the doorway welcoming us. His compassionate look ministered to me because he recognized this was one of the hardest days of my life.

Two of my dear friends asked permission to meet me on that difficult morning—my Bible Study Fellowship leader, who I loved dearly, and Jan's doctor's wife, Arlene, who was also a dear friend. My BSF leader, Carol, had known Jan and me for years, and Arlene had known me since before Jan's birth. Arlene and I went to church together, and she and her husband, Dr. Biehler, were a wonderful godsend to our family. Arlene often kept our church nursery, and for Jan's whole life, she'd been an amazing comfort to me. Here she was again, ministering to me.

I had no idea how desperately I needed both of these ladies that day until I started to fill out the vast amount of paperwork. I couldn't keep myself together emotionally, Carol would hug me and mother me, and Arlene would help me understand and answer the needed medical questions.

It took the entire day to answer all the questions and sign all of the papers. By the time I left, I was totally spent. Walking back in our home, the sound of silence pierced my heart. I could hardly bear it… Jan's favorite music always, always filled our home…and now it played at the Children's Center, and our house felt like a tomb. I crumpled into the floor, my tears and feelings of failure gushing like a river. I wasn't certain I could survive this hard grief of placement!

Over the next weeks, I worried and fretted about Jan, certain that no one could take care of her like me. Guilt kept speaking to my heart, telling me I'd failed as a mother. (You'd think I'd learn the enemy's voice!) My days were spent driving back and forth to the center. Nights I lay awake, wondering if Jan was okay. I'd call the center at 3:00 or 4:00 a.m. to see if Jan was sleeping. Many times, the nurse would put the phone to Jan's ear to let her hear my voice, and I would hear her music playing in the background. I said to Mike, once again, "This is the craziest thing, I can't sleep with Jan here, but I can't sleep with her gone!"

In the midst of all of this heartache, when I was struggling the most, something beautiful occurred. Once again, God's grace burst forth in a very unexpected way.

Ben called from college and said, "Mom, I think I may have met the one." I'd prayed for Ben's mate since he was in the fifth grade, and he'd dated here and there, but he'd never had a serious relationship. I was very excited about his news and looked so forward to meeting this young woman.

Over Thanksgiving of that year, he invited her over to meet us. Her name was Stephanie, and I immediately felt she was the young woman we'd prayed for. But as I'd prayed for her, I'd envisioned a young lady skipping happily through life. Instead, Steph had experienced her own share of heartache. She'd lost her dad when she was six and then lost her mom when she was fifteen. Her sweet stepdad finished raising her and her younger sister. Steph had outlined much of the Bible as she'd learned to cope with her losses. She was a wisdom-filled young woman, and she entered our family's life when we needed her the most.

And talking about God's wonderful graces in my life, she was/is one of the most beautiful treasures gifted to our family. And when she and Ben married in 1997, I was blessed to be an integral part of her wedding plans—shopping with her for a wedding dress, helping pick out her flowers, and I had the privilege of making her wedding veil. God, in His frugalness, brought together a hurting mama that would never be a part of her own daughter's wedding and another of His precious daughters who did not have her mama there to be a part of hers. That still humbles and amazes me today, and once again, God brought our family one of His greatest blessings when we needed it most. I am so humbled by His faithfulness.

Forgive me, I digressed—so back to Jan. As the months clicked by, little by little, I saw wonderful things occurring with Jan. The continuity of care a fresh team of caregivers could provide every eight hours, twenty-four hours a day, did far more for Jan than one tired mom could do, and her health gradually improved. As she grew stronger, so did I. Slowly, I recognized that I was not failing Jan, but I was indeed taking care of her. And I was taking care of her in an even better way than one tired mama could, and I was taking care of me too.

The opened door I hadn't wanted to walk through was a door of deliverance for both me and Jan. That heavy weight of guilt gradually lifted from my shoulders as I saw Jan grow stronger. *Thank You, God, for Your mighty provision for Jan, for me, and for my family. Thank You, Lord, for bringing Steph into our lives when we needed her most.*

And I was actually, for the first time, able to visit Ben at college.

Following Is Yet Another Story of His Grace Keeping Pace:
Jan and Leroy

I was scheduled to teach my Thursday Bible study at 10:00 a.m., and I didn't feel prepared. As I poured over the lesson, a sense of urgency suddenly swept over me. Instantly, I knew I must get to Jan's nursing center.

The urgent feeling was so strong that I picked up my unfinished lesson and my Bible and rushed out the door. Something must be wrong with Jan. Praying as I drove the five miles in congested traffic, I wondered if Jan was struggling to breathe or if she'd spiked a high temperature. The more I thought of the possibilities (the what-ifs), the faster I zigzagged in and out of the morning traffic.

As soon as I reached the center, I jumped out of the car and rushed down the long corridor to Jan's room. To my surprise, Jan was sleeping soundly. No hint of a problem!

I really missed You this time, Lord, I thought. Rather puzzled by the strong urgency I'd felt, I slid into the chair beside Jan's bed. As I watched her sleep, I thought back over the urge in my spirit and was sure I'd been prompted to go to Jan's side. Why?

After a few minutes, I looked across at one of Jan's roommates,

Jennifer. A man I'd never seen before stood over her hospital bed tenderly stroking her forehead. From her labored breathing, her beet-red face, and swollen body, I realized she was dying.

Was this man her dad? He stood alone, slouched over Jennifer, tears streaking down his face. My heart broke as I saw him—a tall, lanky man that looked the part of a tough biker guy, complete with tattoo-covered arms. He wore a sleeveless shirt that sported a bizarre-looking eagle on the front, but at that moment, he looked more like a forlorn boy than a biker dude.

I walked over and talked to him. He told me he was Jennifer's dad and had flown in from California the day before. "I haven't seen Jennifer in a few years," he shared. "I took care of her for a long time after her mama left us. Then as she got older, I just couldn't do it by myself no more," he stopped speaking as his voice cracked.

"Once she came in this center, and I saw they were taking good care of her, I had to find work somewhere. My cousin found me a job in California, and I took it. I couldn't afford to come back and see Jenny. Now they've told me she's in congestive heart failure, and they don't think she'll live but a few more days." He looked away as his shoulders shook, and his voice broke with the emotion of the moment.

We stood silently for a while, and I grieved with him. Then I told Leroy what a blessing Jennifer had been to our lives. She'd been Jan's roommate for several months, and Mike and I visited with her each time we came to see Jan. I told him how much we loved her and that we enjoyed singing "Twinkle, Twinkle Little Star" to her. We loved the smile and the twinkle in her eyes that song always brought.

Leroy's face brightened as he heard about her smiles. A bit of the droop left his shoulders as we talked. Then he asked, "What kind of dog you got?"

Strange, I thought, *how does he know we have a dog?* I'd never seen him before today, and Jan surely couldn't talk to him.

Then his words took me by surprise, "I've almost learned the words to Jesus Loves Me from your daughter's tape."

At that moment, things came into focus.

When I labeled all Jan's clothes for her departure, I also hunted for ways to make the transition easier for her. The week before she left, I made her a special tape. Not only had I recorded many of her favorite songs from her tapes, but Mike and I sang her favorite songs as well. *Jesus Loves Me* was dispersed throughout the tape with our off-key voices singing it. It was the one song that always calmed Jan, so I'd sung it day after day and year after year to her since she was a baby. Since Jan's entrance into the center, that homemade tape played around the clock on her auto-reverse tape player.

I'd recorded the whole family on it...including the dog barking and other background sounds from our home. I'd recorded Mike, Ben, and myself as we barked and quacked on the tape because Jan loved all our silly sounds. It was embarrassing at times because all the kids loved our silly tape and the nurses occasionally put it on the intercom for them all to hear. I can tell you it was a bit humiliating to walk in and hear our off-key singing, but we gladly swallowed our pride to bring a bit of joy to those kids.

Well, poor Leroy had been a captive audience to that off-key singing for many hours, thus the reason he felt he knew our family and me. How it humbled me to think that from that tape, he'd almost learned the words to *Jesus Loves Me.*

After visiting awhile with Leroy, I said, "Leroy, would you mind if I prayed with you?"

His answer was, "It doesn't matter."

Since I didn't know what he meant by that, I prayed with him. Later I found out from the staff that they'd attempted several times to pray with him or talk to him about spiritual things, and he'd firmly rejected their efforts.

Before I left, he also accepted the little *Follow the Shepherd* booklet. It was filled with those scriptures that had gotten me through so many of the struggles with Jan. Once again, the staff was very surprised. Evidently, he'd viewed them as a threat and hadn't let them minister to him in any way. In fact, he'd been hostile to them, but he identified with Jan and me.

I hated to leave him but knew I had to go. I kissed Jennifer on the forehead and hugged Leroy goodbye. With only minutes to get to my Bible study, I hopped in the car and hurriedly sped to the church as tears streaked down my face. In amazement, I pondered what had just occurred.

Only a few days before, I'd complained to God as I also questioned Him, *Why do You keep Jan here on earth? Her body is so twisted, and she's suffered even on her best days. Lord, I don't understand. If You're not going to heal her here, please take her home.*

As I hashed over my thoughts, God impressed these words on my heart, "Pam, there's a plan much bigger than you can see. I knew that Jan could reach Leroy."

I was humbled.

Arriving at my church seconds before it was time to teach the class, I sat in the car long enough to regain my composure. The lesson

God had just taught me was far greater than any I was seeking to prepare for the ladies.

God had used Jan's presence to reach a man who was going through a desperate time in his life. Her tape had opened his heart to His comfort. Jan's life had purpose far beyond what my finite mind could grasp.

And life continued. Ben and Steph were married in 1997, and Jan continued to thrive in her environment of a fresh shift of caregivers every eight hours. Our new normal was sweet.

For Caregivers

As caregivers, our major focus becomes our precious loved ones. Often their needs are great, and when that care turns into years of providing, we can lose sight of the rest of our family's needs as well as our own. I was slowly killing myself in those last couple of years of taking care of Jan, and I thought that was what I should do. I also didn't want to listen when observers or friends said, "I don't think you can continue to do this." Finally, I prayed and asked God.

He opened a different door—one I'd never expected to walk through. That door was provision for Jan, me, and my whole family. I now see that if we, as caregivers, push beyond our own limitations, and we lose our health, our whole family has lost. I had to learn to accept the unexpected door of provision because it was totally different than my plan. I typed Psalm 91:11 and placed it over Jan's bed where ever she was, and it brought me so much comfort: "For he will order his angels to protect you wherever you go" (Psalm 91:11, NLT). In fact, all of Psalm 91 is an amazing comfort. If you're drowning in responsibilities, I encourage you to ask God and listen for His sweet leadership—He will make a way for you.

God Grace Keeping Pace

I believe God has countless plans for our lives. Jan's life testifies to that, and she couldn't walk, talk, or use her hands. One of His greatest tender mercies comes in seeing the glimpses of His grace dispersed throughout our lives. His goodness and grace overwhelm my heart.

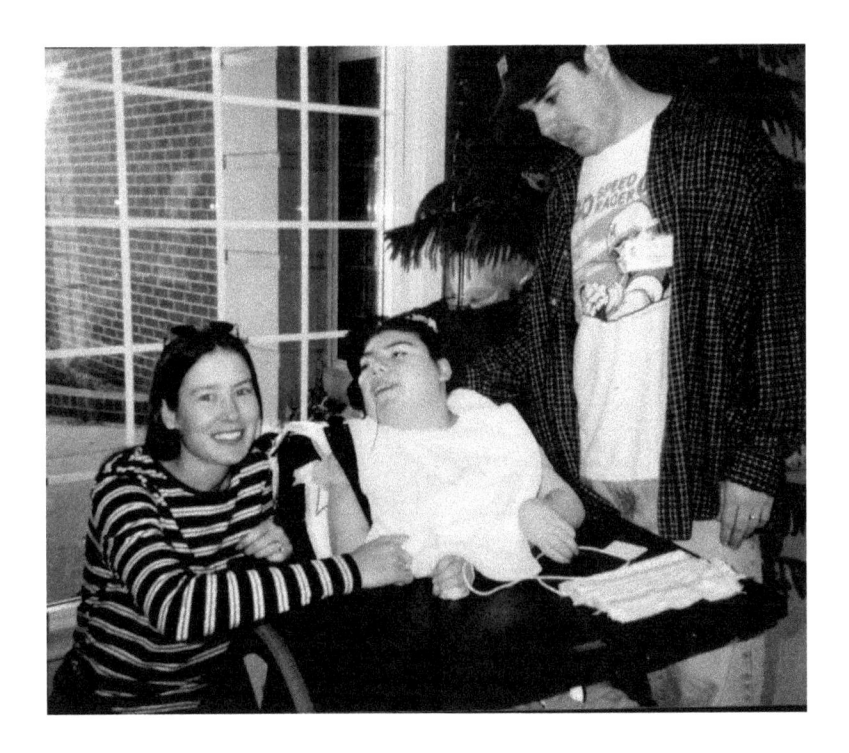

Chapter 20
THE ANCHOR HOLDS

"And I will give you treasures hidden in the darkness—secret riches. I will do this so you may know that I am the Lord, the God of Israel, the one who calls you by name" (Isaiah 45:3, NLT).

The spring of 2000 dawned with more heartache than I thought I could bear. In March, my oldest brother, Wayne, died suddenly of a heart attack.

My sister Lynda was diagnosed with a reoccurrence of melanoma only six months after Wayne died and was instantly thrown into a vicious fight for her life. The day I received her sad news, I was standing beside Jan's bed at the Children's Center, already crying. I'd just found out we were going to have to move Jan to an adult nursing facility when Lynda called. I was doubly devastated. Two thousand was certainly turning out to be a rough year.

Jan's 1994 placement at the Pediatric Nursing Center had blindsided me, but hindsight had allowed me to see that it was a wonderful blessing for both Jan and me. I'd grieved her absence from our home, but I'd continued to be an integral part of her care at the Children's Center. I wasn't prepared for her to move into an adult facility far from me. Coupled with the loss of my brother, two surgeries myself, and a move from our home of twenty years, I was struggling emotionally already, but with the news of my sister's battle and Jan's move, I was a mess.

This move came because of another Federal Government mandate that required that all children twenty-one years and older be removed from the pediatric nursing center. Jan would turn twenty-one in January. That meant we had to find an adult nursing facility for her. I already knew that when any of our critical care children left the care of the center, they averaged only living about six months—unless they'd gone to Corn, Oklahoma. Corn was a tiny town in Western Oklahoma. It had a post office and an old building that at times was open for coffee and sandwiches, and that was about it. It was almost a two-hour drive from our home. The thought of Jan being so far away seemed inconceivable to my heart, but I searched and found there were only a handful of facilities near us that would take a patient as young as Jan, and particularly one that was as critical care as Jan was. I learned which ones were willing, and then I made no appointments but visited totally unannounced at odd times of the day. I found situations that were totally unacceptable to me. I also learned that I could look up nursing homes online on a federal site and find their ratio of nurses to patients and their ratings and check for bad reviews. It confirmed what I'd found at the nursing homes I'd visited unannounced. That site helped me greatly in my decision-making.

I was told about one facility that was only about two miles from our home. I checked their reviews, and inspections were very good. I visited it, unannounced, and was impressed with their facility….it was clean and well-staffed, but they had no openings. They put us on a waiting list but gave us very little encouragement. It was the only adult facility I found acceptable—I cried my way through the others, knowing I couldn't entrust Jan's care to them. In one place, I saw chains around each chest of drawers and all the bedside tables. When I inquired about it, they said that there was a theft problem there and everything had to be locked up. I'd been in a car wreck in 1997, so I could no longer lift Jan as I had when she and I were younger, or our solution would've been simple, we'd have brought her home. So, one fall day in 2000 found my sweet daughter-in-love, Stephanie, and I following an ambulance to Corn, Oklahoma. I sat in the back seat of the car with our 2000 July blessing, four-month-old grandson, Jack, and I cried much of the way—particularly when I saw how far off I-40 Corn, Oklahoma, was. It seemed we were driving to the middle of nowhere! I couldn't understand, and I questioned God greatly and grieved yet another unwanted change in our lives. Would I ever learn that I could always trust His heart?

Amazingly, much of Mike's drilling that he was doing for a major client moved to the area around where Jan moved. (And those oil leases had been leased years before). Because the nursing home was in an isolated area, they provided two-bedroom suites at their facility for families of their patients to rent. They were nice and equipped with a fully furnished kitchen, and they only charged twenty dollars a night. We rented one of those apartments almost every week and stayed one or two nights. We could roll Jan down to our room and let her hang out with us. Mike and I spent much quality time together and with Jan—because the distance he normally drove daily ate up enormous amounts of his time.

We also found out why the care was so excellent—many of the aids and nurses were from the surrounding Mennonite farm community. Jan resided there for two years. One of my memories is that when 9/11 occurred, I was driving back from Corn on I-40 after having been there for a couple of days. I remember listening intently to the developing saga as I drove. Another precious memory is talking to my sister on the long drive back from Corn. She died in March of 2001. Jan's care at Corn was so excellent that I felt comfortable to spend the last week of Lynda's life with her in Alabama.

In 2002, Jan became very ill and was sent to a small hospital in Weatherford, Oklahoma. After a week there, she was transferred to Baptist Hospital in Oklahoma City and placed under the care of a pulmonary specialist. Jan was in that hospital for a total of fifty days. After I'd sat behind her in her hospital bed twenty-four hours a day for over twenty days, once again, I was so exhausted that I could barely stand. I was coming to the end of my strength and ability. I cried out to God for help once again, and the next morning, as I read my Bible, God answered.

He gave me a scripture that said He'd send help from His sanctuary. I didn't know what that meant because we'd recently moved, we were in a new church, and we knew few people there. Besides, Jan was now twenty-four years old and was almost more than I could handle physically, and I was accustomed to taking care of her. I wondered how anyone could help us.

But as always, God's grace kept pace. My friend, Gay, called, and her sister Fran, the one that took me to Kenneth Hagin's healing school, the one who is a nurse, wanted to drive from Lawton and take a couple of nights with Jan so I could rest. I was amazed. Keep in mind that this was a time before Facebook or social media, so these people coming together had to be God. One of Jan's original babysitters from the early years of Jan's life was called Angie Yager Culbertson, and she wanted to take a few nights. She drove from Owasso, Oklahoma. Gay wanted to take a few nights, and she drove from Dallas. Sweet

Stephanie insisted on taking a few nights, too, even though she was pregnant.

He did indeed send help from His sanctuary…He mobilized His saints to help a tired mama and a little girl who were in desperate need. I went home and showered and slept in my own bed. Without their sacrificial gift of love, I don't think I could have handled those fifty days. Those sweet saints had answered His nudge with love and care and became His sanctuary of provision for Jan and me.

During that time, it became necessary for the doctor to do a tracheotomy on Jan so she could breathe. That meant Jan could no longer live at the Corn facility. Once again, I cried out to God. I had no idea where she'd be able to go. The places before we chose Corn were limited, and that was without a tracheotomy. With a tracheotomy, it would be nearly impossible to find a good place for Jan. I talked to the specialist about our predicament, and he asked, "Is there any place you'd like for her to be?"

"We've been on a waiting list at Oklahoma Christian Home in Edmond for over two years, but they've never called us back. It's only two miles from our home. He smiled broadly and said, "I just happen to have gone to high school with the chief Administrator there, and he's one of my best friends—let me give him a call. He picked up the phone, called, and incredibly Jan became the first twenty-four-year-old with a tracheotomy and a feeding tube ever accepted as a resident. What are the odds of us getting the one doctor who knew the head administrator of the only facility we were interested in?

Jan moved two miles from our home and was placed on hospice. Shockingly, only two weeks later, Mike found a knot under his arm. "My times are in thy hand" (Psalm 31:15a, KJV)

God's Grace Keeping Pace

When you're blindsided by life, keep looking for those glimpses of God tucked in your hard. They are always there. He sent us help from the sanctuary when we had no idea how He could provide; He did it! *Lord, give us eyes to see the hugs You send in our difficult places of life and let us glimpse Your graces that are always there.*

Chapter 21
IT IS WELL WITH MY SOUL

"I will go before thee, and make the crooked places straight"
(Isaiah 45:2a, KJV).

While showering one evening in May of 2002, Mike found a knot under his arm that hadn't been there the evening before. We made an appointment, saw a doctor, and had a biopsy. And as we waited patiently for the results, the call finally came.

"Mike, it's doctor Deck. He wants us both on the line—the results of the biopsy are in." Mike picked up the phone nearest me.

"Mike, I'm so sorry, but the tests were conclusive—it's malignant melanoma."

Mike grabbed his chest in disbelief, and I thought I'd pass out. We were stunned. That's what my sister had died of only thirteen months earlier. We'd already fought this beast and lost. Certainly, Mike couldn't have it, too, but he did.

From the beginning, as shocked as we both were by the diagnosis, we both agreed that this did not blindside God, and we clung to Jan's scripture that God had given us twenty-five years earlier when we knelt at Children's Hospital, praying desperately for her.

You made all the delicate, inner parts of my body,

    and knit me together in my mother's womb.

Thank you for making me so wonderfully complex!

    Your workmanship is marvelous—how well I know it.

You watched me as I was being formed in utter seclusion,

    as I was woven together in the dark of the womb.

You saw me before I was born.

    Every day of my life was recorded in your book!

Every moment was laid out

    before a single day had passed.

Psalm 139:13–16 (NLT)

And with that scripture and many others in hand, we marched forth into yet another unwanted battle. Mike never pitied himself, nor did he give in to fear, nor say, "Why me?" He literally showed us how to live in Christ and how to die in Christ. I was and am so proud of him. Now I was a bit of a different story. I was strong for him, but when he was asleep, I battled greatly with fear. I let those what-ifs overpower my faith. I wondered how I could live without him. I'd left my parent's home at nineteen, and we'd walked beside each other for thirty-three years. I couldn't imagine life without him, and I didn't want to imagine life without him. We'd spent twenty-four years of our lives fighting for Jan's life, and we'd just become grandparents and were totally in love with our new role.

I pleaded for God to heal Mike. And it appeared by Christmas (2002) that Mike was responding well to the treatments. But we went in for a routine CAT scan on Christmas Eve, and a few days after

Christmas, we received another difficult-to-hear-telephone call. The cancer had spread to Mike's brain. He was only fifty-four and had always been very healthy. His prognosis now looked very bleak.

Mike and I talked into wee hours of the morning that fateful night. Most people don't survive long after melanoma crosses the blood-brain barrier, and sadly, we knew that firsthand—from my sister's ordeal.

In spite of this devastating news, Mike exuded peace, and that comforted me greatly. He said, "What it is, it is. What is hardest for me is that it looks like you and Ben are going to have to bury Jan without me."

In all the years we'd fought to keep Jan alive, we'd certainly never imagined this scenario. In fact, we'd bought burial plots when Jan was twelve because of her poor health, never once imagining that Mike would be the first one to need a plot.

Mike continued to ask God to heal him, but he also prayed, "Lord, if You're ready for me to come home, I'm ready, but there're a few things I'd like to ask of You. You tell us to share the desires of our hearts. I'd love to be here when this next grandbaby is born." Ben and Stephanie were expecting their second child in April.

"And, Father, I'd like to see Jack turn three." Jack was our firstborn grandson, and we both adored him. He was the reason we'd moved to Edmond. We had enjoyed every second of the extra time we'd had with him.

Because we already knew the havoc this particular cancer can cause to the brain, Mike also prayed, "And, Lord, I'd like to keep my mental capacity so I can keep working. I want to pay off this house." We'd bought a new home in 2000 to move closer to Ben and Steph.

Our old home in Oklahoma City was paid off, but we'd taken a loan on the new one, planning to pay it off quickly.

Mike had always been a very good money manager. The oil business was/is either feast or famine, so he'd saved since we were newlyweds so we could navigate the oil field famine times. It was just like him to have this heart's desire and voice it to God.

Mike underwent brain surgery twice. He had a tumor plucked from a high real-estate area of his brain, and another grew back in the same area in only six weeks. He underwent yet another brain surgery in February to get that one. He came out of surgery each time very alert with all of his brain functions in tack. It was amazing. Actually, it was miraculous.

Sadly a few days after the second surgery, he experienced seizures and was told he could no longer drive. That was the only time I saw his spirit crushed by bad news. His engineering work involved one hundred to three hundred miles of driving daily. When I saw his devastated look, I told him if he was brave enough to ride with me, I'd be honored to be his chauffeur. He smiled and accepted my offer. I was blessed to have had that privilege for over six months, and I loved that extra time with him.

His oil field buddies were a wonderful blessing too. That week in April, when our second grandson was born, one buddy called and said he wanted to drive Mike to work all week so I could help with the baby. Another of his buddies gave me my own personal key to a restroom at an oil field company that was in the area we traveled. In a bind, I could discreetly go there for relief because, generally speaking, there were no bathrooms on the locations or ones I'd feel comfortable to use. I loved to brag that I was probably the only grandma in the Western Oklahoma oil field who was chauffeuring around her hubby to various oil wells with her own personal restroom key tucked in her wallet!

Mike's buddies also tried to meet us along our route for lunch wherever we happened to be. One of my fond memories is meeting some of them at an old folk's community center for a home-cooked meal. Another is of me and Mike. I got us stuck in one of those cow path oil lease roads that led through deep soft sand. Mike said, "Move over, gal." He got in the driver's seat and backed that Suburban up and gunned it, and out we came.

I'll share a story I wrote in my journal during one of our oil field adventures:

The Oil Field Adventure

Transcribed from my journal:

With detailed directions in hand, we travel miles down a paved country road somewhere near Taloga, Oklahoma. At the fork, we turn and travel three and three-quarters miles until we see a gravel road.

I turn down it, following the written instructions carefully, and immediately the terrain changes, and so does the road. We encounter many chugholes (chugholes, not potholes!) Chugs are bigger than potholes, in case you are wondering. You do not want to hit one of those.

I drive carefully, dodging those craters and praying that we won't meet a big oil field truck because if the chughole was in the wrong place, there wouldn't be room for the two of us to meet.

Then the crater-filled dirt road narrows again to only

one lane—a sandy, curvy cow path tunneled through the middle of tall trees, weeds, and wildflowers. I am amazed by the beauty surrounding the path, but I surely don't want to meet a truck now. We bounce across a cattle gap as the path twists and turns and goes deeper into the woods. I am fascinated.

Then we entered a very hilly stretch—very hilly for Oklahoma, and I spied a big oil field truck coming our way. Thankfully, I saw a place in a field where I could pull over and wait for him to pass.

Then we return to the narrow winding path. We round a corner, top a hill, and all of a sudden, the oil field location bursts into view. It was literally dug into the side of a hill, then smoothed into a very flat and level location, totally covered with white pea gravel and gypsum rock that glistened in the sun. The location appeared stark, framed on all sides of that white gravel by Oklahoma's red dirt. In the center of that location stood a gleaming engineering feat—a huge metal oil rig—standing tall and proud against Oklahoma's amazing blue sky. Wow.

What a site for this grandma to behold. I was also amazed as I thought about it—we'd rounded the corner in the middle of seemingly nowhere as we'd followed those handwritten instructions, and there we'd found a crew of men working hard—drilling for Oklahoma crude.

Mike hopped out of the Suburban to check on the operation as I sat in the vehicle and wrote what I'd just witnessed.

> Mike would have Gamma Knife surgery on Thursday—a surgery to zap yet two more brain tumors as he literally fights for his life, but today he was doing what he loved. How blessed I was to share this experience with him. I was filled with praise and thanksgiving as I pondered it all.
>
> We'd followed those detailed instructions to the oil rig—those precise instructions led us down a narrow and, at times, forbidding looking path, but as we rounded that final corner, there lay a shiny, leveled, safe clearing with men hard at work.
>
> God's Word was very detailed instructions, too, on how to navigate life. I felt He'd just allowed me to experience the following of the instructions in the natural. We'd seen a lot of beauty along our path in spite of the chugholes and dusty road, and we'd arrived safely at our destination as we'd followed those thorough directions. I felt His comfort embrace me because He'd just showed me firsthand that whatever lay ahead for us, if we'd keep following His instructions, He'd guide us safely to our destination.

By April, Mike was between chemo treatments when our second grandson was born, and he was able to enjoy baby Will's birth. He also asked three-year-old Jack in late June what he wanted for his July birthday—his answer was "a park." That translated to a swing set.

Mike shopped online for that gift and settled on one that he thought would last. It was delivered shortly before our grandson's birthday, and Ben put it together with the help of three-year-old Jack. Mike was delighted to get to see Jack play on that swing set as we celebrated his third birthday.

Then he proudly paid off our house on July 1, and we continued our oil field treks through July 26. By then, Mike had had two brain surgeries and three Gamma Knife surgeries, and with seven new brain tumors, he was still doing calculations in his head that most people must have a calculator to do. On August 6, it became almost impossible for him to walk. He used that confined-to-bed time to type letters on his old laptop to the two grandsons and to me. What an amazing treasure he gifted us.

To the Grandsons, he wrote:

> By the time you boys read this, Pawpaw Mike will be in heaven with Jesus. We found out a year ago that I had cancer, and as hard as I have fought it, it looks like it's going to get the best of me. My prayer was that I would live to see Will born and see Jack's third birthday. God has allowed me to see both of these things.

And then he shared some family background with them...and then wrote,

> Boys, my prayer for you is that you will both love the Lord with all your heart and serve Him. I was raised in a church, and I knew a lot about God, but I did not have a personal relationship with the Lord until 1971, when I prayed and asked Jesus into my heart. Boys, placing God first in your life will be the most important thing you will ever do.

And that is the most amazing heirloom that Mike left us, praying for his grandsons to accept Christ and sharing with them how important it was to his life. And between his letter writing, he received visits from his oil field buddies from Oklahoma City and from all over Western Oklahoma. Big burly guys would walk up our front steps, traipse back to our bedroom, say their goodbyes, and leave crying as they walked back down our front steps as they left. Mike fought it hard, but on August 8, 2003, I called hospice. I'll share a few of the wonderful ways God comforted me in the days that followed. Remember, God's grace always keeps pace with whatever we face!

His Grace Keeping Pace

When my sister was diagnosed with a reoccurrence of her melanoma in 2000, I researched everything that I could find about that deadliest form of skin cancer. I'd found very helpful info on a website called Melanoma Patients Information Page (MPIP), and I hung out there a lot, researching and reading what had worked for others. Their logo was the hummingbird, and I'd researched why.

I'd found that hummingbirds are the smallest bird on earth. Aerodynamically they aren't supposed to be able to fly. (Thankfully, they don't know that!) And, not only do they fly, but they are the only birds that hover in place, fly backwards, sideways, and upside down too! They can't walk or hop. They weigh less than a nickel and drink twice their weight daily! They aren't able to smell, but they see colors vividly—and are very attracted to red and orange. And, the ruby-throated flies non-stop over the Gulf of Mexico—500 miles during migration, eighteen to twenty-two hours on a non-stop flight! Isn't that amazing?

My sister died in 2001, but it was the early August of 2003 when I first saw hummers in my own yard. I was sitting in our den in Edmond as I tearfully filled out the hospice paperwork for Mike. I could hardly believe he was dying of melanoma too. My heart was broken, and I felt numb. I thought I couldn't face this loss too—and as I sat grieving, two hummingbirds flew to the window and hovered…peeking right at me.

I was so surprised that I asked the hospice nurse if she saw them! I thought perhaps in my pain, I was seeing things. She assured me she saw them too! It was a huge hug of hope to my weary heart.

They left, and I didn't see them again until a couple of days before Mike died. I'd run outside into our flower garden to cry, and suddenly two hummers hovered directly in front of me—in my heart, it was as if God said, "It'll be okay."

I felt strengthened and hugged by God once again—His grace was keeping pace. And it would serve me well for the rest of my life because from that day forward, every time I see a hummingbird, I'm reminded if they can do the impossible, so can I. After all, I was designed by the same Wonderful Creator!

"I [and you] can do all things through Christ who strengtheneth me [you]" (Philippians 4:13, KJV).

His Grace Keeping Pace in Loss

Even though I'd filled out all the hospice paperwork, I really didn't want them to come. It meant death was knocking at our door, and I didn't think I could face it.

But on a hot August day, our hospice person arrived. I sat visiting with her feeling very numb, recalling that only the year before, I'd done a similar interview for Jan. It seemed surreal, like a dream, no make that a nightmare, that I was filling out that same paperwork yet again, and this time for my beloved Mike.

I'd interviewed this same hospice for Jan, and they had given her good care. Mike had seemed so healthy when I'd filled Jan's paperwork out only a year earlier. Numb and emotionless and in disbelief, here I sat—with Mike and Jan both dying.

Mike's caregivers were a totally different crew than Jan's. Our assigned nurse was Ruth. We immediately liked her. She was a pastor's wife and had just started this new position with hospice. In fact, we were her first clients. Mike and she hit it off wonderfully. They had several theological discussions about the Bible in their short time of knowing each other, and we quickly developed a sweet relationship.

Ruth told us that she'd come a couple of times a week, and as Mike's condition progressed, she'd step up her visits. What none of us could've known on her first visit was that Mike's condition was going to progress very rapidly. Blood clots began to form in his feet and legs, and Ruth would only get to be his nurse for a little over two weeks.

On her second visit, Ruth realized that things were moving far faster than she'd dreamed. She sat down with me at our kitchen table as she chose her words carefully. She only spoke a few words before she burst into tears. She was embarrassed and apologized profusely for crying and losing her cool. I assured her that her words hadn't taken me by surprise because I could see that Mike was declining rapidly. I also assured her that her deep care had touched my heart mightily and comforted me as I hugged her and thanked her.

On Monday night, August 18, Mike woke me up and said, "I just want to tell you how much I love you and tell you goodbye. Tell the kids I love them." My arm was across him, and I could feel his heart pounding. I said, "How do you know you are leaving?"

"I see Jesus!"

I asked him to describe what he saw, and he said he saw Jesus surrounded by millions of beautiful lights. We lay holding each other, and as time went by, Mike and I both fell back asleep. When Mike awoke the next morning, still in his pain-ridden body, he was upset and questioned, "Why did I see Jesus, and then He didn't take me with Him?" He was more than ready to go.

We went back to the Bible and read many scriptures…among them, John 3:16 (KJV): "For God so loved the world that he gave his only begotten Son, that whosoever believeth in him should not perish, but have everlasting life." And another one, 2 Corinthians 5:1–2:

> For we know that when this earthly tent we live in is taken down (that is, when we die and leave this earthly body), we will have a house in heaven, an eternal body made for us by God himself and not by human hands. We grow weary in our present bodies, and we long to put on our heavenly bodies like new clothing.
>
> 2 Corinthians 5:1–2 (NLT)

And Mike was comforted and smiled and, with a sigh of relief, said, "God made it easy, didn't He?"

"Yes, He did. He paid the price, and praise God, He paved the way for us to spend eternity with Him." We were both so thankful that His gift didn't hinge on us being good enough, or kind enough, or smart enough—but totally depended on His provision of laying down His sinless life. He had freely bridged the way for us and for anyone and everyone who called on His name.

God's grace kept pace that last week of Mike's life in ways I could've never imagined—from hummingbirds to roses, to visits, and to random people sent by God to help walk Mike home. I'll share a few: My brother, Jerry, and his son-in-law, Brett, visited from Mississippi that last week. I'll always remember Brett buying groceries and cooking for us that weekend. Then on Monday, hospice delivered the hospital bed, and it was up to us to move Mike into it. My brother, Mike's brother, and my nephew were able to do that.

And my dear friend, Ginger, normally keeps a very full fall schedule, but God had other plans for her that fall. She is a professional storyteller and a sought-after speaker for classrooms as she made the Oklahoma land run and many historical truths come alive to students across our state. For some reason, as her schedule booked up for that fall of 2003, she kept the week of August 18 open, turning down several invitations for that week. She didn't know why, but she felt a nudge in her spirit to keep that week free. She found out why when she came to our home on August 18. She realized Mike was dying, and she could be there for us that entire week. She drove the forty-five minutes from Yukon each day and spent it with Mike and me when we needed her most.

As the week progressed and things became increasingly harder, a variety of friends called to say they felt led to spend the night with us. All week, someone was with us at one time or another—godsent friends—who loved on us, cooked for us, sang hymns with us, and dried our tears. Even now, I'm amazed and humbled when I think about it. I never asked a person for help but asked God, and He provided richly.

"Now unto him that is able to do exceedingly abundantly above all that we ask or think, according to the power that worketh in us" (Ephesians 3:20, KJV).

And this next wonderful provision of grace still makes me cry. On the Thursday before Mike died on Friday, God graced us with the sweetest of provisions.

Another God's Grace Keeping Pace Moment

"Mike, what's wrong?" I'd just walked into the bedroom and saw that he was in extreme pain.

"Pam, all of a sudden, I can't stop moving my legs." I rushed to the hospital bed where he lay, and to my shock, I saw his legs sliding back and forth over the sheets. We hadn't been on hospice long, but his health was deteriorating rapidly. His legs and feet had started to swell in the last few days and were now almost doubled in size. Test results showed the cause to be multiple blood clots. Nothing could be done.

As the blood clots multiplied, movement of any kind became horrendously painful. In fact, Mike hadn't been out of bed for three days and normally lay as still as possible, being careful to not move his legs.

With the onset of this out-of-control movement, pain and despair were written all over his face. I tried to keep my composure, but I was near hysteria, knowing that this unexplained movement was causing him such great pain. I felt helpless. My friend, Ginger, had just left. Unlike at the hospital, I had no button to push for help and no nurse down the hall to call.

I grabbed the phone and shakily dialed the hospice number. A terrifying thought raced through my mind as I waited for someone to answer. *Was this new symptom coming from a progression of the can-*

cer in the brain? "Help us, Lord, and please don't let this be the brain tumors." *What if I was losing him mentally too!* "Lord, Lord, please help us," I prayed out loud.

My urgent prayer was interrupted as hospice answered the call. I explained our situation and gave them directions to our home. The problem was, we needed help now; they were forty-five minutes to an hour away. Mike's situation was getting more painful by the second as the involuntary movement continued. He also began to express his fear, "Pam, I am afraid this is being caused by the brain tumors!" That concern seemed to make his restlessness much worse.

In the midst of our crisis, the doorbell rang. "Mike, I'll be right back," and I ran down the hallway and threw open the door. I couldn't believe who was standing there—one of my neighbors who happened to be an RN.

Debbie lived on the corner only five doors down from us. Over the past year, as I walked the neighborhood in the cool of the day, I'd stopped on several occasions to admire her beautiful rose garden. We'd share our faith and bits and pieces of our journeys. I'd told her of our plight with cancer, and she shared that she'd recently lost her dad. In fact, the large rose garden she was planting was in his honor. (Later, she told me she normally did not take an evening walk at dinner time but felt very impressed that evening that she needed to.)

Now, here she stood on my front porch with a handful of those roses. The smile on her face quickly faded as she looked into my panicked eyes.

"Pam," she said, "what's wrong?"

Before she could finish her sentence, I grabbed her arm and pulled her down the hall toward the bedroom, explaining as we went,

"Debbie, I've never been so grateful to see anyone in my life. Mike is having a terrible episode of some kind, and I don't know what to do!"

As soon as she got to Mike's side, her training as an RN kicked in. She assessed the situation quickly.

"Mike," she said, "I suspect you're having an allergic reaction. Have they changed any of your medications?"

"Debbie, when the nurse was here this morning, she gave him a new pain patch. She said it should control the pain more consistently than the oral medication."

"Do you have the box the patch came in?" I ran to the trash and quickly found it. Debbie immediately dialed the pharmacy of the hospital where she worked.

"I need to know the possible side effects of this medication?" as she reeled off the list of ingredients to the pharmacist. Before the conversation was over, they had determined that the patch was the culprit of the uncontrollable movements, and we removed it. I still had liquid morphine, and she told me to give it to Mike. Thankfully, long before hospice arrived, Mike was over the worst of the pain and was resting.

As Debbie rang the doorbell on that August evening and stood waiting with her beautiful gift of roses, God had a much bigger assignment for her than her gift of roses. What started as an act of kindness was actually a miraculous answer to prayer. Not only did Debbie help a suffering saint in his final days, but she aided his weary caregiver at a moment when I needed it most.

Another Grace Keeping Pace in Provision

Thursday night, our dear friend June came at bedtime and spent the night with us. I'd kept Mike's favorite praise music playing in his room all week, and she and I sang along with it many times that night as we slept very little. Her sweet prayers over Mike and me brought much peace to us both.

The next morning, Friday, August 22, Ruth came, and hospice sent an additional nurse with her because they knew we were close to Mike's homegoing. Ruth, herself, stayed as long as she dared that day, well after her shift was over, but ultimately, she had to leave. She had young children and a family waiting at home. Within two hours, I called hospice again because Mike was dying. Ruth wasn't allowed to come back. Later I found out as she drove home, she'd requested to be allowed to return, but her wise boss wouldn't permit her to because he knew she'd become too involved emotionally. I didn't think I'd ever see her again.

When Mike drew his last breath on August 22, 2003, all three of his prayers had been fulfilled, and he was at peace. He'd seen our second grandson born, he'd celebrated Jack's third birthday, he'd kept his mental capacity, and he'd been able to continue to work and pay off the house. God had answered all his requests. He was surrounded by family and friends as he breathed that last breath on earth, and I know he took his next breath in heaven as he walked through that amazing Door called Eternal Life. I'm so thankful that death for the Christian is the Door to Eternal life—The Door—Jesus Christ. Hallelujah! And at his funeral, we played his three requested songs, "It Is Well," "How Great Thou Art," and "I Can Only Imagine."

On an icy wintery night almost three years later, on my mom's ninety-second birthday, February 17, 2006, Jan died. Hospice was called to record her time of death. Ruth, Mike's hospice nurse, was on duty that night, and when she heard the name, Jan Whitley, come across the radio, she told her co-workers that she wanted to go on that call.

As I sat waiting for the ambulance, the door opened, and in walked Ruth. She looked angelic to my grieving heart as she walked directly to me and threw her arms around me. And said, "As soon as I heard Whitley come across that intercom, I knew it was my call." What a wonderful comfort she was.

And I've found throughout my life that God has always, always sent His mercy and grace in one way or another when I've needed it most. This time it was via one of His servants named Ruth. And when I asked God why Jan died on my mom's birthday, He said, "Your mom has prayed for Jan's healing more than anyone else in this world. I healed Jan on her birthday!" What a comfort that was for me and my mom to hear.

Jan and Mike are buried side by side in a small cemetery, Olive Hill, that sits by the home we lived in for twenty years. We bought those plots in 1990 when it appeared Jan wouldn't live through the winter. Amazingly she saw sixteen more winters—living to be twenty-eight. We never once dreamed Mike would be buried there first.

At Jan's funeral, we played a Sandy Patty song called "Masterpiece." It is the words to Psalm 139:13b–14a (NLT): "[…] and [You] knit me together in my mother's womb. Thank you for making me so wonderfully complex"—the scripture read long ago to us—the young couple kneeling and praying at Children's Hospital.

And that sweet cemetery sits on the hill above the dugout where Ben used to play. The same dugout where some of the people who made the land run are buried—the ones that thinking about their struggles gave me courage to face mine. My name is etched on the monument, too, that marks their grave.

I'm still living in the dash—the time after entering this world before graduating to heaven. I look forward to my graduation day when I, too, walk through that beautiful Door. I can't imagine how glorious it will be to see my Savior face to face and to see Jan whole, walking and talking with Jesus, and to be reunited with all of those who have gone before.

"Weep Not"

At the dawning of this new day,

My thoughts were on you.

At first there was a sadness

As I thought of what you were going through.

And then from within, I heard, "Weep not."

For today is his/her graduation day!

Graduation from a life of limitations,

Graduation from all fears and pain,

Graduation from all sickness

Graduation, never to suffer again.

Weep not, my child, today is his/her graduation day,

He/she's robed in a gown of glory.

He/she strolls through streets of gold.

He/she sings with the angels,

He/she walks with the King,

His/Her joy overflows, weep not!

Pam Whitley Taylor

God Grace Keeping Pace

His grace has kept pace so beautifully throughout my struggles and losses. I can't list them all because they are too numerous, but I've shared my most precious ones. In the midst of the pain, there was always a grace tucked sweetly in—from hummingbirds to people, to scriptures, to roses, and those graces came when I needed them most, just as Corrie ten Boom's dad said, "When I boarded the train of despair. Let's never stop looking for those beautiful godsent glimpses of His marvelous grace."

Chapter 22
WHEN I'M GONE

"It is the glory of God to conceal a thing: but the honor of kings is to search out a matter" (Proverbs 25:2, KJV).

Those first years that followed Mike's death were very difficult. I'd left my folks home to marry when I was nineteen, and I'd never lived alone.

Mike and I'd moved in 2000 to a new home as well as to a new church so that we'd be near our grandkids. Overnight, with that shocking cancer diagnosis, I watched our dreams slowly crumble around us, and I found myself living in our new home with the loudest silence I'd ever faced. I felt I was a stranger in a foreign country. Not only was Mike gone, but my sister was gone, and Jan was on hospice. There was no normal to go back to anywhere in my life. As painful as it was, God continued to meet me each step of the way.

At first, I barely functioned. I lost weight because I'd forget to eat. Then I read a sweet writing by Elizabeth Elliot, and it helped me greatly.

Elizabeth and her husband, Jim Elliot, were new parents and had just gone overseas as missionaries when her husband was murdered by the very natives they were attempting to reach. (There's a movie about that—*The End of the Spear*.) She was in a foreign land with a new baby when suddenly she became a widow. I can't imagine. She, too, found it very hard to function. She learned to ask herself, "What is the next thing that I need to do?" Many times, her answer was as simple as "change the baby's diaper."

I learned to ask myself that same question multiple times a day, and sometimes the answer was as simple as "eat lunch" or "pay the electric bill" or "get the mail." Surprisingly, that question helped me to function. If you are grieving, you might want to try this tip. It will help you.

Then I was invited to GriefShare classes, and that also ministered to me greatly. I took the thirteen-week course four times because I was too numb the first thirteen weeks to absorb much. Each time I took it, I gathered more tools for the healing of my heart. It also afforded me the opportunity to meet other widows who were my age. That helped me to not feel so alone, and I'm still friends with many of those ladies today.

The GriefShare video series takes into account that grieving people have short attention spans. Please consider checking in to that program if you're grieving. Google GriefShare and put your zip code in the form they provide, and hopefully, you'll find a class near you. I understand that DivorceCare is equally as good, should you be walking there.

I learned during those days that there was no easy shortcut to heal my pain. After all, I had to learn a whole new life because half of me was gone. I tried to rush it by moving to a different home. That didn't help. I learned gradually that single or widow was an unwanted title I had to learn to embrace.

As I watched the GriefShare videos, I realized many things had brought me grief throughout my lifetime that I'd not identified as grief. I'd grieved when I moved from Mississippi. I'd grieved when I saw my childhood home grow musty and in disrepair. I'd grieved when our little dog died. I'd grieved terribly with the placement of Jan, but again, at that time, I'd not identified it as grief. We'd certainly grieved when Mike was diagnosed with cancer.

And I looked back to one Sunday morning in 1984 when I'd gazed over the congregation after two couple friends (the kind that stick closer than a brother) had moved away within weeks of one another. I felt their absence so keenly that I'd cried for a few weeks each Sunday morning in church. I now recognized I was grieving their absence.

Identifying those emotions called grief helped me understand myself and my life journey in so much better. As people, we grieve so many things other than death—loss of jobs, loss of health, loss of friendships, loss of abilities, loss of dreams, any major life changes—like moves or unexpected twists that our lives take—the list goes on and on. It helps to be able to recognize the emotions connected to grief.

And for me, my hardest and most difficult grief thus far has been the loss of Mike. For me, it was like trudging through a deep and dark never-ending tunnel, and it took me a long time to see light at the end of that long dark tunnel. During that time, I faltered and made mistakes as I tried in my own strength to find a new place to belong and fix my pain. I ran from the extreme pain and hurt that I dealt with daily as my hurting heart was more broken than I thought possible.

Finally, I surrendered it all to Him and stopped running and stopped trying to fix it myself. I found out that God doesn't waste our tears or our sorrows when we let them go and lay them at His feet. Here're a few of the things I jotted down that I learned during my hardest grief journey.

- Grief can paralyze and can cause temporary memory loss and forgetfulness.
- Grief can be so heavy that you feel it weighing you down.
- Grief can bring a feeling of desperation because of the many gaping gaps left unfilled.
- Grief can affect health—too little sleep or too much, weight loss or weight gain, heart palpitations, extreme fatigue, etc. I couldn't eat much for several months and became too thin.
- Grief brings ambushes when you least expect it—a surprise attack of tears—a wave of grief.
- Grief and hard losses forever change us—we'll never be quite the same.
- Grief has purpose: God promised that He would work to our good, what Satan meant for our evil/our downfall. I had to learn to trust Him on that as well.
- Grief is never without hope—I had to learn to recognize that.
- Grief should only be for a season; God doesn't want us stuck there.
- Grief equips us to be comforters—perhaps this is one of the most beautiful and purposeful outcomes. "Grace and peace to you from God our Father and the Lord Jesus Christ. […] who comforts us in all our troubles, so that we can comfort those in any trouble with the comfort we ourselves have received from God" (1 Corinthians 1:2, 4, NIV).

Thankfully, God was faithful every step of the way, when I failed and when I got back on track. So many people helped me heal too. My dear friend, Brenda, called me every Sunday night for over two years. Her mom had been widowed at my age, and she understood how hard it was. Stephanie and Ben helped in many sweet ways.

All the firsts were hard, and Steph knew that. I flew to Mississippi by myself for the first time after Mike's death, and I dreaded coming back into my empty house late at night alone. She took pics of the boys, made posters with little funny things the boys said and posted them on the garage door going into my house, then down the hall where she knew I'd walk. When I pulled in the dark garage that night, oh my, how I was blessed by her thoughtfulness. And in the midst of my pain, God continued to minister to me in the sweetest of ways. Below, I'll share several snippets of God's grace keeping pace:

His Grace Keeping Pace That First Christmas:
In Pieces

It'd be my first Christmas in thirty-three years without Mike. I shopped for flowers for his new tombstone, as others shopped for Christmas tree ornaments and decorations. I sorted through the remnants of his life as others prepared for family get-togethers. Surely, I could do something constructive in the midst of such awful pain.

When I walked into our closet, memories flooded my soul as I saw five of Mike's favorite shirts. When Ben was in college in the early 90s, the big flannel shirt became the fashion craze. I purchased two or three of those big heavy shirts for Ben for Christmas. Every time he came home for the weekend, Mike would raid his closet and come out wearing one of those shirts with a mischievous smile.

It became a joke, and for the next few years, I bought Ben and

Mike identical flannel shirts for Christmas. Ten years later, those shirts continued to be Mike's favorites. In fact, as he started chemo and had fever, he wore one of them most of the time.

So, as we headed into the holidays, I took those shirts off their hangers one by one. I hugged them close as I walked upstairs to my sewing room and laid them in a corner. I wanted to do something special with them. It took a few days to get the courage to cut into them. Perhaps dismantling them bore too much of a parallel to what had happened to our lives.

I was determined to make a treasure for Ben. I studied the shirts and measured them. I could get several eight-inch-wide strips from the front and the backs of the shirts as well as from the sleeves—if I could bear to cut them apart? I forced myself to precede with more than a few tears.

I cut the eight-inch strips first and then cut them into as many squares as I could. Then I began to sew the squares back together as a quilt began to emerge.

As friends looked at my work-in-progress, they commented on how great my color combinations were. I hadn't chosen the colors. They were all of his shirts, and together they formed a beautiful coordinated palette. It seemed impossible to finish my project by Christmas, but I was determined. I wanted desperately to do something special for Ben, and I knew that was it. I asked God to give me the strength to complete my project, and day by day, the quilt grew larger.

I sewed the labels of the shirts on some of the squares and deliberately cut strips with pockets so that it would always be evident that the quilt was made from Mike's shirts. To finish the project, I bordered the quilt in navy flannel and quilted the shirts with my machine in a free-hand-motion style. I was able to move the quilt around under the needle so that I could stitch names.

I stitched Whitley, 2003, Mike, Pam, Ben, Steph, Jack, and Will into the borders of the quilt. I envisioned one day our grandsons searching for the names hidden in the design and Ben sharing fondly the memories of his dad and the shirts

On Christmas Day, as our son opened his gift, tears welled up in his eyes. The look on his face blessed my heart. And the grandsons grew up loving Pawpaw Mike's blanket made from his flannel shirts.

I knew God desired to do the same thing with our lives. If we'd give Him the shattered pieces, He'd make us whole again. We'd have a new look and a new purpose, created from precious remnants of the past. Tips for future keepsakes:

- Look for items of your loved one that can be repurposed treasures for yourself or your family. My boys have Pawpaw Mike's old handkerchiefs, and I made Stephanie a bookmarker out of remnants of her mom's things. She carried it in her Bible on her wedding day.
- I've seen leather boots, leather belts, leather purses, and wallets made into treasured keepsakes. One friend had her mom's purses cut into beautiful crosses for the wall. I wish I'd thought of this because Mike had some wonderful leather cowboy boots.
- I've seen favorite shirts made into pillows, quilts, teddy bears, or aprons. T-shirt quilts are quite nice too.
- Write down precious memories for future generations—that will become a great treasure

- Celebrate your loved one's birthday each year by recalling special and sweet memories. I know someone who fixes their loved one's favorite dishes on the date of their homegoing. Keep the memories uplifting and celebratory—not sad and weepy.
- Make special boxes of random things they owned—I share an example in a story below.
- Have jewelry made using the loved one's copied signature or cards where they've written: "I love you." I've seen those messages and others embedded in bracelets or necklaces.
- I've seen a grandma's handwritten recipe framed and hanging on the kitchen wall.
- I made Christmas ornaments from a tattered old quilt of my grandmother to share with her grandchildren. I made an old pieced-together quilt top (never quilted and not big enough to be a quilt) into a Christmas tree skirt. I admit I'm a very sentimental person, so I love these things.
- Old costume jewelry can be made into numerous things. I had an old cultured pearl necklace of my mom's restrung into a new keepsake for me. I've seen old brooches grouped together on velvet to form a shape like a tree or heart and then framed. I've seen that done with an antique button collection as well. It's healing to be creative in turning our loved one's mementos into treasures.
- Don't get rid of things too quickly because later, you may regret it.

I'll share the following story in case it gives you, my sweet reader, ideas:

Treasure Boxes

"Why are you keeping that junk?" friends asked. I wondered myself. Since the death of my husband, Mike, I'd downsized my home by seventeen-hundred-square feet. Moving twice had forced me to sort through the remnants of our thirty-three years of marriage and give away office furniture, my husband's sports equipment, clothes, multitude of books, and many of his tools. I'd saved his collections and keepsakes and held on to a lot of seemingly silly things. I say silly because friends and family who'd seen my can't-part-with stacks asked why I was keeping them since they couldn't possibly serve any purpose. He'd kept those trinkets, and I guess I felt I should too.

I crammed my unique assortment into two purchased boxes, one a black square box with a lid and the other a large lidded round cardboard box. I stashed one in my closet and another in the guest room closet. Maybe one day, my grandsons would enjoy some of the random trinkets those boxes contained and remember their grandpa. I forgot about them.

Then one Friday night, about five years later, my six-year-old grandson Will spent the night; I took him shopping and let him pick out a toy. He chose a spy kit. Once home, we put the spy gadgets together, and we created a game. I hid an old rhinestone piece of jewelry in my closet and wrote out clues to help Will find it. Armed with his new spy flashlight, he searched for the loot.

During his hunt, he discovered one of my stashed boxes of stuff. He was fascinated by its contents: three old watches, key rings loaded with once purposeful keys, golf balls, a coin-filled medicine bottle, six antique cigarette lighters that were Mike's granddads, and a variety of other things—from old cuff links to tie tacks to bullets. Will spent an hour looking at the items, asking about each one. Then he looked up at me, his blue eyes sparkling, "Mimi, do you have any more treasure boxes?"

Smiling, I led him to the guest room, and I revealed the second box. It delighted him more. It held a variety of pocket knives, a letter opener, a little set of tools, old belt buckles, his grandpa's engineering calculator, and two items that particularly fascinated him—wind-up alarm clocks. He explored the contents for another hour and then wanted to look in the other treasure box again.

The next morning, when his mom arrived to pick him up, Will immediately said to his three-year-old brother, "Mimi has treasure boxes! Ya wanna see?"

He proudly took his brother to look at the newfound treasures.

As I pondered how enchanted my grandsons were with those two boxes, I was so glad I'd saved that seemingly frivolous stuff. Pawpaw Mike's odd collection turned out to be a little boy's treasure and delight...and his grandma's too! It did indeed have purpose.

Lord, help me to recognize the seemingly useless parts of my life that You want to use. May I give them all to You and allow You to repurpose them into treasure to bless others.

His Grace Keeping Pace at Easter

The week before Easter (2004) was filled with delightful spring weather, but Saturday dawned with a chilling drizzle and dense fog. From my warm spot in bed, I turned the TV to the weather channel—the weatherman predicted a freeze for that night. Reluctantly, I shoved back my warm, fuzzy comforter and slipped out of bed. Walking to the window, I peeked through the blinds and shivered as the Oklahoma winds pounded the cold rain against the glass. I felt like the day looked—gray and dismal.

This would be my first Easter in almost thirty-three years without my husband, Mike. He'd died of cancer six months earlier, and all of the firsts since his death had been painful—his birthday, Thanksgiving, Christmas, Valentine's Day, my birthday, and now Easter. The absence of his presence was excruciating and tainted each celebration.

Pulling on my robe, I walked to the kitchen to make coffee. I peered at the gloomy day as the wind whined around the corner of the house. My gaze settled on Mike's vacant chair at the kitchen table. I dreaded another holiday. I didn't look forward to the empty space that would be beside me in tomorrow's service either.

My mind skipped to lunch I'd prepare for my son and his family and to the treasures I'd planned for our grand babies' Easter baskets. Last year, Mike delighted in hiding the Easter eggs and carving the ham. Tears welled up in my eyes. *Oh, Lord, will I ever be content without Mike?*

I poured my cup of coffee and returned to my bedroom. Plumping the pillows against the headboard, I crawled back under the warm covers and grabbed my Bible. I turned to the Psalms and read verse 10. The first verse touched my heart so much, "O Lord, why do you stand so far away? Why do you hide when I am in trouble?" (Psalm 10:1, NLT)

I read it again.

I cried, *Lord, I feel just like this. You seem so far from me. I don't understand.*

Though I wanted to pull the covers over my head and stay in bed, I knew I'd better get ahead of the holiday crowds and buy the groceries for my Easter meal. I exchanged my Bible for a notepad and listed the things I needed to do. Then I pulled my jeans on, grabbed my umbrella, and headed to the store.

Once again, I missed Mike terribly. We typically went out for breakfast on Saturday mornings and then drove to Sam's Wholesale Club. The trip concluded at the Sam's gas station as Mike put gas in my car. He insisted on pumping the gas long after brain tumors rendered him unable to drive.

Today, I thought, *I'll get the gasoline first since my gauge was near empty.* As I pulled into the pump area, my cell phone rang. With the distraction, I failed to see that two young people—a guy and a gal—stood beside the gas pump where I stopped.

I looked up and thought, *Oh great, just what I need—someone who wants money to wash my windshield.* Maybe I could back up, but I glanced back, and two cars had already pulled behind me. It was too late. I fumbled through my wallet for my Sam's card and braced myself for their sales pitch as I stepped out of my car.

"Good morning." The young woman cheerfully handed me a business card that had her church's info on it.

"We're here on behalf of Real Church." Her brown eyes sparkled, and she pointed across the street to their building as her long brown hair blew in the cold wind.

"We're here to tell you that God loves you, and we want to fill your gas tank for free."

Surprised, I protested, "I am a Christian, and I love the Lord. I don't want you to spend your money on me. Please use the money for the next car."

"You're exactly who we want to do this for."

I hesitated and then sat back in my car, leaving my door partly open. They swiped their credit card, and the young man pumped my gas.

"This is so kind of you and your church."

"Our congregation wanted to do something special this Easter for the neighborhood. One of our members had this idea and donated the money," the young lady said with a smile as she pushed her wind-tossed hair out of her face.

"We'll fill up tanks until the money is gone. We want to tell as many people as we can that God loves them."

I thought back to the Psalm I'd read earlier. I recalled my statement to God about being far away, and the tears started to trickle down my cheeks.

I looked at the young man and said, "I want you to know that God sent you to stand in my husband's shoes today." My voice quivered as I struggled to get out the rest of my words. "My husband died last fall, and this is my first Easter without him. He'd normally be pumping the gas for me. You'll never know how your kind gesture has blessed me."

"Ma'am, I'm honored to have this privilege," he said as his voice broke.

I hugged them both before I drove away. The day no longer seemed dreary. I knew God wasn't hiding from me. He was waiting to bless me through two messengers stationed at a gas pump with His message, "I love you."

"It is the Lord who goes before you. He will be with you; he will not leave you or forsake you. Do not fear or be dismayed" (Deuteronomy 31:8, ESV). *Lord, thank You. You never leave or forsake me. You are there in the dark and dismal days, waiting to fill me again.*

His Grace Keeping Pace the Second Christmas without Mike

Would I ever enjoy a holiday again? The year before, I'd skipped the Christmas Eve services at our church because it was my first holiday without Mike. He'd died in August, and all the firsts were difficult. I'd thought the second year would be easier, and I attended that service with my son and his family.

Seated in the audience beside them, I looked at the beautiful scene before me—the stage was filled with hundreds of white candles flickering against a backdrop of numerous lighted Christmas trees. Carols that I usually loved to hear played in the background. Unfortunately, my focus wasn't on the beautiful occasion but rather on the couple-filled church and the empty seat beside me. That empty spot seemed to shout that Mike was gone. The joy and wonder of the birth of Christ normally caused my heart to soar, but on this night, I felt very alone without my Mike, and the service brought more pain than joy to my grief-stricken heart. I struggled to hold back my tears and asked God to help me find joy again. I was glad when the service was over.

After the service, Ben and Steph rushed to get my two grandchildren from the nursery. We'd head home to share our Christmas Eve meal together. When we picked up the nineteen-month-old, it was obvious that he was very cranky. It was well past his dinnertime, and he was not only hungry but he was tired as well. As soon as we were in the car and buckled him into his car seat, his fussiness increased. It looked like it would be a long ride home.

In an effort to calm him, my son asked, "Will, tell Mimi what the lion says?"

Will growled in the deepest voice he could muster, "Eeeatttttt," and we all giggled. That delighted Will.

"Will, tell Mimi what the sheep says."

"Eeeeeatt, eeeeeeattt, eeeeeattt," was the next sound that he bleated forth, and the smile on his face said volumes—Will loved being our entertainment, and thankfully, that trumped tired and hungry.

"Will, tell Mimi what the dog says."

Will barked out, "Eatttt, eatttt, eatttt."

Soon I was laughing so hard that tears spilled down my face, and the entertainment and laughter lasted the whole trip.

By the time we arrived home, my spirit was much lighter, and for the first time in a long while, joy had inched its way into my heart and into our celebration too. I gave Will a big hug as we walked inside and quickly breathed a prayer of thanksgiving, not only for my precious grandkids but for my loving Father, who'd heard my prayer and answered it in an unexpected way.

His Grace Keeping Pace in Change

In 2007, Ben accepted a job opportunity that moved him and his family to Owasso, Oklahoma. It's a town just outside of Tulsa and was 117 miles from where I lived in Edmond. By then, boy number four had arrived, and I adored them all. I made that drive so often that my kids invited me to move to Owasso, and I took them up on the invitation and moved in 2009. I told Ben then if he was anything like his daddy, he might want to make a job change, and I didn't want him to feel that he couldn't move because of me.

In 2010, Ben had a wonderful opportunity to make a major career change. It involved many weeks of training hundreds of miles away from home. He'd graduated from his program in the fall and began a new career that involved law enforcement. I was thankful I was in Owasso because while he was away for his training, I was able to help Steph with the four boys, and I enjoyed every grandma moment.

After graduation, his new career path led them to move across the country. The week before they moved, it sunk in that Ben, my only remaining child, could now be in harm's way. I suddenly was filled with terrible fear and anxiety, and I cried out to God.

Once again, God spoke to my heart, saying to take a look at Ben's high school class ring.

My first thought was, *I have no idea where his class ring is.*

And I felt God impress on my heart once again, *Yes, you do. It's in the wooden jewelry box in the bedroom.* I walked into the guest bedroom where several of Ben and Steph's things were stored while their house was on the market, and on the dresser sat their jewelry box. I opened it, and amazingly, on top sat Ben's high school class ring. I picked it up and held it up to the light.

At the time Ben ordered his high school ring, he had planned to become a lawyer but changed his mind while in college. Engraved in that stone was an emblem of the scales of justice—an identical emblem that was now imprinted on his badge. After I'd cried for a while and thanked God over and over for His mighty faithfulness, my anxiety vanished. God was in control, and I knew no matter what, I could trust Him with it all. That class ring was another of His graces keeping pace with this mama's anxious heart. Oh, Father, You are the

Name Above every name.

Another of His Graces Keeping Pace in My Future

When I initially moved to Owasso in 2009, I wanted to find a ladies' Sunday school class. I called the church where I planned to attend to ask them about one. They gave me a name—Linda Melone—and I called her. Linda told me all about her wonderful Sunday school class, invited me to it, and then added, "But it is not a ladies' class; it is a singles' class."

I definitely didn't want a singles' class—and I told Linda that. She insisted, however, that I wanted to be in her class. She'd lost a daughter and was widowed as well, and she loved that class. And soon, Linda had me wanting to meet the people that she loved. I visited and loved them too and joined. That class was exactly what my hurting heart needed.

After morning and evening church services, we usually all went out to eat together or to someone's home. Our motley crew was made up of widowed and divorced singles, as well as a couple of married couples who had once walked in our single shoes. For those of us who lived alone and had little or no family near, this class met so many needs. Those meals shared together were lifelines for those of us who now ate most of our meals alone.

On a Sunday evening in May of 2010, one of the married couples brought a single gentleman with them to another of our after-church get-togethers. His name was John, and over barbecue brisket, I asked him about his slight west coast brogue. He said he'd moved to Oklahoma from California in 1992 but that he was born and raised in Barbados and moved to California when he was nine.

He returned the following Sunday to our group, and he soon became one of our regulars. From then on, he and I visited from time to time in Sunday school and over meals as our class continued to dine together. As Christmas approached, I thought of how hard the holidays must be for him, and before I knew it, I'd invited him via a private message on Facebook for a home-cooked meal. As soon as I sent that invite, I wished I could reel that request back. He accepted my invitation and months later told me he was just as nervous as I was when he answered yes. Funny, he'd not wanted to be in a singles' class either.

When the evening arrived for that meal, I was a basket case. *What had I done—inviting him to have dinner with me?* As I tried to cook that meal, I was so nervous that it took three trips to the grocery store to get all the ingredients. On the first trip, I left one whole bag of groceries at the checkout, and the next trip was made to pick up that bag. Then back at home, as I started to actually cook the main dish, I realized I'd forgotten the key ingredient—the chicken. That third crazy trip left me barely enough time to prepare the meal. Oh my!

But over that meal, John and I talked and talked. Our stories were similar—lots of heartache and loss. Soon we were talking often on the phone and sharing almost every meal together. By March of 2011, we were engaged, and in April, we traveled to Mississippi so he could meet my mom and my brother before our May wedding.

My mom was ninety-seven. She'd suffered a stroke when she was ninety-two, and we had sorted through her belonging as she opted to move into a nursing facility. Her few remaining belongings were stored in boxes at my grandparents' old farmhouse where my dad had grown up—my brother now owned that land and had restored the old house. He lived about fifty miles away but used that house as a place to take Mother when he was visiting her and a meeting place for people like me when we came into town to visit my mom. It was a delightful place to visit, filled with memories. On this visit, my brother graciously pulled his fifth wheel to the property for John to stay in, and I stayed with my brother and his wife in the farmhouse.

The next day we brought my mom to the farm, and we all shared a meal together as everyone became acquainted. In the midst of our visit, my mom asked me to fetch her a hairbrush from one of her stored boxes. When I reached in the box, I also found an old scarf that my brother had sent to Mother in 1969. It was a scarf with the Island of Barbados stamped on it. You see, my brother was assigned a four-month job stint in Barbados when I was a senior in high school.

Mother had moved four times since that forty-two year ago present; she'd left the farm, moved to a duplex, then to a one-bedroom apartment, and then to a nursing facility. Every item she owned had been carefully sifted through, and the few items that remained now resided in those boxes. I couldn't imagine what the odds were that she'd still have that Barbados scarf—but there it was! I was so surprised that I cried as I brought it out to show my "fiancé from Barbados" and my mom.

I believe that God knew before the foundation of the world that in their twilight years of grief, a Mississippi girl would meet a Barbados boy, and He'd blessed them with something that linked their past. What a sweet and dear blessing from our Heavenly Father. Thank You, precious Lord.

John and I were married in 2011, and we will celebrate eleven years of marriage in May of 2022. God is so faithful in His graces. "God places the lonely in families" (Psalm 68:6a, NLT).

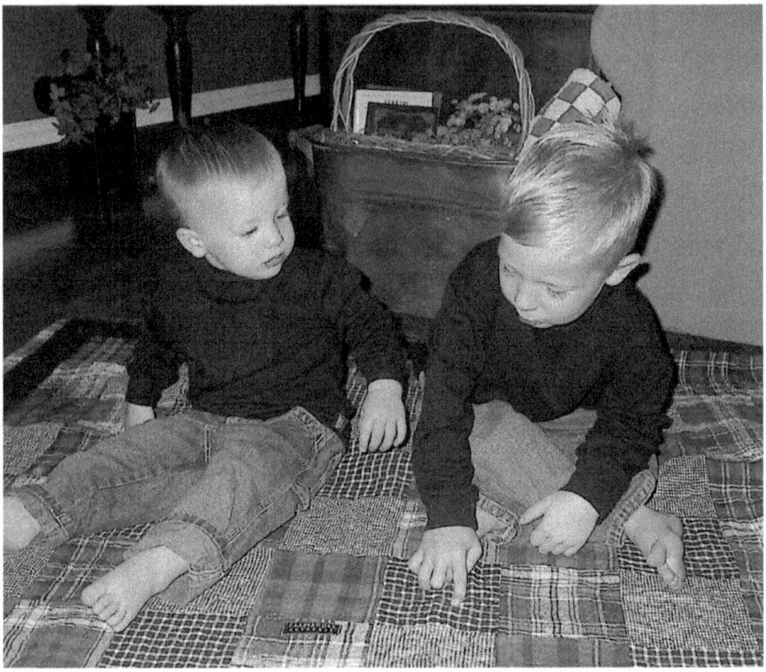

Chapter 23
THE MERCY TREE

"For whatever is born of God overcomes the world. And this is the victory that has overcome the world—our faith. Who is he who overcomes the world, but he who believes that Jesus is the Son of God" (1 John 5:4–5, NASB).

As I admired my and John's cup collection, my attention was drawn to our beautiful handmade pottery bowl displayed on the shelf beside them. John and I purchased it on a trip to Colorado a couple of Christmases ago. I picked up the bowl and ran my fingers around the smooth navy rim and explored the bottom of the bowl. The artist used shattered and crushed windshield glass to add a unique beauty to the bottom of his creation. The bottom is smooth and glazed, but the once useless glass shimmers and shines from beneath its sheer seal. Its beauty drew us when we bought it, but I was also fascinated by how it was crafted.

My eyes teared as I realized the bowl represented a lot more than our trip to Colorado. It personified our lives—mine and John's. They were shattered and crushed, too...yet our Creator took our brokenness and did a marvelous new thing in our lives.

When John and I first married, because of my caregiving years, I'd seen no national parks. Together we have now adventured in our RV to thirty-seven parks, including several in Alaska. And John taught me a new skill, photography. We've memorialized those adventures with pictures, mugs, bowls, and Christmas ornaments.

Each morning when we drink our coffee, we're reminded of where we've been, both figuratively and in our travels. We know all too well that life is fleeting and can change overnight. We hold hands often, say "I love you" daily, and explore the world around us when we get the chance.

And those mugs sit in the midst of our home, surrounded with my things and his, reminding us daily of how God's grace is allowing us to walk together in our later years. God took that which was broken, mended it, repurposed it, and bought forth unexpected beauty, just like in our shattered windshield-glass bowl.

Lord, may we never become complacent with what You have granted us today.

God's Grace Still Keeping Pace at Seventy

In my old age and in my late in life marriage, I've taken up a new hobby—photography. Both of my God-given daughters, Stephanie and Angie, already were great photographers, John had been a great one most of his life, and he and they inspired me. John supplied me with a good camera, and after I took my first up-close butterfly picture, I was hooked.

We live on a bit less than two acres of land, but it is treed and backs up to a green belt with stream. As we feed the birds, we've recorded over fifty varieties in our yard, and we've photographed most of them. I see this as a huge God-given grace for me to have time to smell the roses.

The Dreaded Pile—Blessing of Grace

Behind our property lies a beautiful, tree-filled easement. It is home to a stream, multiple huge rocks, and a variety of critters. In the midst of that rugged beauty stands an ugly row of electrical lines. Every two or three years, the county drives trucks and heavy equipment behind our fence to clear and chop anything that has encroached on those electrical lines.

I dread hearing the roar of their equipment because I know the aftermath will be untidy piles of broken and crushed limbs thrown in huge ugly heaps. I also don't like that it scares our wildlife and dislodges some of the critters from their homes. I understand the unwanted pruning is necessary to prevent power outages when we have our Oklahoma ice storms and high winds! But this past winter gave me a new perspective.

During the cold of the winter, I look for the occasional warm day to pull up one of our old green plastic chairs and sit in that easement to breathe in the God-given beauty—and to photograph anything of interest.

On one winter day, as I sat very still, I noticed that one of the ugliest, tallest brush piles was filled with activity. I zoomed my lens toward the movement and discovered both male and female cardinals hopping, climbing, and fluttering beneath the protection of the rotting pile, and then I saw juncos, white-throated sparrows, and wrens as well. They flew in and out of the heap…using the piled-up limbs as their little ladders. What a blessing to witness!

That which I'd dreaded provided me a cleared spot to sit and witness a wonderful lesson—an ugly pile of trashed twigs and limbs had become a bed and breakfast of rescue and protection for my small feathered friends! What I'd viewed as destruction had become their provision.

Focus

On one warm July morning, I sat quietly on our front porch glider and glanced around the front yard. The neighbor's persimmon tree stood tall as it was slowly being encased by tent worms, my butterfly plant bowed from old spent flowers—my Arizona blanket plant suffered the same problem. What I was gazing at looked rather ugly.

But then in flew a beautiful hummingbird. And five minutes later, an amazing swallowtail glided onto the remaining flowers on the butterfly plant. I thought about Philippians 4:8 (NIV): "Finally, brothers and sisters, whatever is true, whatever is noble, whatever is right, whatever is pure, whatever is lovely, whatever is admirable—if anything is excellent or praiseworthy—think about such things."

As always, I had a choice to make, and I chose to focus on the birds and butterflies—not the tent worms and dead flowers!

Our world is that way. We have a choice minute by minute as to where we place our focus. Will we focus on what is wrong with our lives and our world and those we love, or will we focus on what is right? God, may I always turn my focus to You and the beauty before me. May I view this world through Your lens, Lord, not my limited vision—and may I keep praising You in all things.

Summing It Up

Seventy-one years have come and gone since my journey with God began. Like Job in Job 42:5 (NLT), I can say, "I had only heard about you before, but now I have seen you with my own eyes."

I see His gentle guidance and loving care each step of the way, and I can face the future knowing that He will continue to lead me throughout my numbered days. He is the One True God who knows the end from the beginning and gives us His living hope in the midst of each step. We can trust Him with it all.

Recalling this scripture (one more time) where Joseph says to His brothers, those same brothers who sold him into slavery, in Genesis 50:20a (KJV): "But as for you, ye thought evil against me; but God meant it unto good." May each of you remember always there is nothing, nothing, nothing that God can't work to your good. Our part is to obey what He says in His Word, His instruction book, forgive whether we feel like it or not, love like God loves, and then give Him all of the messes, mistakes, and the broken pieces of our lives and watch expectantly as He works it all to our good.

More Lessons That Have Graced My Life

- Life is short. Let's embrace today and count our many blessings.
- We can delight in the fact that Jesus Christ is the only One who is the same today, tomorrow, and forever. Let's praise Him for that.
- Life often does not seem fair, but it is still good. Let's praise Him no matter what.
- Let's choose always to do the next thing. No matter how simple that next step is, with Him, we can do it.
- Let's choose to move forward and let go of our pain.
- Our giftings will bring us energy and joy—let's try to use them daily.
- Let's always remember God loves us…Period. He won't love

us less when we fail or more when we think we've done it right.

- Let's remember that painful things are stepping stones to growth and will make us better if we don't allow them to make us bitter.
- Let's take joy in the fact that God can use everything in our lives, but only we can choose to give Him all those hurts and broken pieces.
- Let's not be anxious for anything. Anxiety will rob us of our health and our joy.
- Let's remember that we are never too old to grow and make changes—let's allow the Holy Spirit to direct our paths out of our pain and darkness.
- We can't control what trials come into our lives, but let's react to them with eyes of faith.
- Fear focuses on our dire circumstances, but let's choose to look with eyes of faith, filtering it all through His Word.
- Let's not walk as victims, but let's walk in victory as overcomers.
- Let's see the difficulties we face as God's miracles that haven't happened yet.
- Let's keep a positive attitude and look for opportunities in all things: A negative attitude finds woe and fault in everything. Let's keep looking upward.

Thank you for taking the time to read our story, and I pray that God's grace keeps pace with whatever you face. Blessings to you and much love.

> The fundamental fact of existence is that this trust in God, this faith, is the firm foundation under everything that makes life worth living. It's our handle on what we can't see. The act of faith is what distinguished our ancestors, set them above the crowd.
>
> Hebrews 11:1–2 (MSG)

My God-given daughters—Stephane and Angie

John and I headed to Alaska

ANGELS BY MY SIDE

Ben and Mike

Stephanie Whitley

My mom—Pearl Powell

Lynda Basye—my only sister and her two daughters, Nicole and Rhodona

Jerry and Jessie Powell and their two daughters, Teresa and Sharon

Wayne and Mary Powell and their children, Barry and Shelia

Rev. Jack and Phyllis Poe

Larry and Arlene Biehler

Ginger and Zane LaCroix

Gay and Andy Wilkinson

Ken and Gail Yager

Angie Yager Culbertson

Fran Ihler

Lori Biehler Brannan

Bill and Brenda McCuin

June and John Cromling

Penny and John Stover

Art and Velma Poe

Carolyn and Danny McHenry

Donna and Jerry Broughton

Diane and John Yakel

Christy Yakel Chappell

Paula Biehler

Janice Craig

Jolynn Craig-Heath

Judy and Jack Craig

Miriam Foster

Susan Wright-Wallace

Anita Wright

Rose Coffee

Travis Watkins

Kay Garr

Carol Cutler

Judith Hilbun

Jana Hlavaty Windsor

All of my wonderful patterners

Toni Lamb

Lynda Baylor

Helen Foster

Cheri Fuller

Susan McCall

Don and Bette Creel

Danita Testerman

Diane Janney

Lynn Steele

Ruth Buchanan

Judy Stipe

Sue and Randy Ferguson

Paula Hemingway

Jack, Will, Sam, and Max Whitley

The Institutes staff

The Ladies' SS Class of Highland Hills Baptist Church

The members of Highland Hills Baptist Church

The Lakeside elementary staff

The entire staff of the Children's Center

The Corn Nursing Home staff

Oklahoma Christian Home staff—now Bradford Village

A multitude of nurses and doctors

And since 2011—John Taylor

And Brett and Angie Shepherd

CPSIA information can be obtained
at www.ICGtesting.com
Printed in the USA
JSHW052247170123
36254JS00003B/11